EMERGENCY
PRAYERS

Deborah Smith Pegues

HARVEST HOUSE PUBLISHERS

EUGENE, OREGON

Cover by Koechel Peterson & Associates, Inc., Minneapolis, Minnesota

EMERGENCY PRAYERS
Copyright © 2008 by Deborah Smith Pegues
Published by Harvest House Publishers
Eugene, Oregon 97402
www.harvesthousepublishers.com

ISBN-13: 978-0-7369-2246-3
ISBN-10: 0-7369-2246-6

Printed in the United States of America

08 09 10 11 12 13 14 15 16 / BP-NI / 10 9 8 7 6 5 4 3 2 1

*This book of prayers for crises is dedicated to
all the faithful intercessors who stand in
the gap for the needs of their families, friends,
country, churches, coworkers, and all others
in their circles of concern.*

Acknowledgments

Special appreciation goes to the following individuals who prayed for me, submitted prayer focus ideas, evaluated the prayers contained here, inspired me by their example, or just cheered me on to the finish line. This book would not have come to fruition without your support. Thanks a million: Raynae Soo, Mamie Leonard, Marlene Talley, Frank and Bunny Wilson, Elvin Ezekiel, Joshua Smith, Cheryl Martin, Billie Rodgers, Eula Smith, Delissa and Kelvin Kelley, Dana Smith-Lacy, Pamela Johnson, Redelia Fowler, Pamela and Alvin Kelley, Wilfred Graves, Oscar Owens, Harold and Ruth Kelley, and LaTonya Pegues.

As always I appreciate the flexibility and inspiration of my editor, Peggy Wright, and the entire dream team at Harvest House Publishers.

Finally, words could never express the extent of my gratitude for Darnell, my husband, and his unwavering love and support for all I do.

Contents

Part 4: Prayers for Children and Relatives in Crisis

Part 5: Prayers for Relationship Crises

Part 6: Prayers for Financial, Business, and Legal Crises

Part 7: Prayers for School, Job, and Work Crises

Part 8: Prayers for Emotional Crises

Part 9: Prayers for Church, Country, and Other Crises

Praying the Word of God

Prayer is perhaps the most talked about, written about, and least practiced spiritual discipline. The lyrics from Irishman Joseph M. Scriven's popular hymn, "What a Friend We Have in Jesus," are a vivid reminder of its importance.

> Oh, what peace we often forfeit,
> Oh, what needless pain we bear,
> All because we do not carry
> Everything to God in prayer!

Prayer is the oxygen of our spirit; our survival depends upon it. We must always pray and not give up (Luke 18:1). In order to be equipped for an enemy attack, we must do as the psalmist declared, "Evening, and morning, and at noon, will I pray, and cry aloud: and He shall hear my voice" (Psalm 55:17 KJV).

Nothing drives us to the throne room of God like trouble. Further, nothing develops our spiritual muscles like the exercise of faith during the crises of our lives. Notwithstanding, my greatest concern in writing this book is some readers may consider it a license to pray only during such times. Let me say at the outset, this book of scripturally based emergency prayers is not meant to be an escape hatch during a crisis for those who do not have an existing relationship with the Lord. When you fail to regularly protect yourself with the umbrella of prayer, you will surely get soaked with the inevitable rain of trouble. In his suffering Job lamented, "Man who is born of woman is of few days and full of trouble" (Job 14:1).

The goal of this book is to provide a tool that will show God's children how to declare the Scriptures in the form of a prayer in times of trial, testing, temptation, or distress. Praying His Word assures us we are praying His will. He is on constant watch over His Word to perform it (Jeremiah 1:12).

Let me caution you not to be appalled at and question the appropriateness of my including certain prayers that deal with blatant or even detestable sins. Know that God's children are still human and often fall into the same temptations as those who walk in darkness. Prayer is our defense as well as the route back to God's straight and narrow path.

In the interest of time and space, I have started each prayer at the *petition* stage. However, we must remember that if an earthly father wants to be praised and appreciated before being bombarded with a request, how much more should we honor our heavenly Father in this way? Therefore, in each instance of prayer, be sure to enter into His gates with thanksgiving and into His courts with praise; be thankful unto Him and bless His name (Psalm 100:4). An opening phrase as simple as "Lord, I thank You for the privilege of coming boldly before Your throne to obtain mercy in this time of need" is sufficient in a crisis. Why? Because during your noncrisis devotional time, you have worshipped Him for His omnipotence, omniscience, and omnipresence.

While I encourage you to review this book often and memorize selected prayers that focus on your particular crisis, I will caution you to resist the temptation to reduce your prayer to a rote exercise. I strongly suggest you take the time to look up each biblical reference given in the prayer and meditate on the related passage. Feel free to modify these prayers to apply to various individuals and circumstances on behalf of others when the issue is not one you are personally experiencing. Most of all, when you approach your heavenly Father, always expect a positive result to your prayers. Come believing. Know that "without faith it is impossible to please Him, for he who comes to God must believe that He is, and that He is a rewarder of those who *diligently* seek Him" (Hebrews 11:6, emphasis added).

I challenge you to come up higher in your faith and to stop operating at "see level"—believing only what you can see. Yes, you know that God *can* answer your prayers; believe that He *will*. Take courage and strength from the words of David: "In my distress I prayed to the LORD, and the LORD answered me and set me free" (Psalm 118:5 NLT).

Part 1

Prayers for Spiritual Crises

I Want to Be Saved Now

Father, this is a spiritual emergency for I need salvation. I acknowledge I have sinned and come short of Your glory (Romans 3:23). Thank You for demonstrating Your love to me in that while I was still a sinner, Christ died for me (Romans 5:8). Your Word says that Jesus is the only door to the Father and I must come to You through Him alone (John 10:9).

I repent of all my sins. Please forgive me, Lord, and come into my life now. I confess with my mouth that Jesus is Lord and believe in my heart that You raised Him from the dead. According to Your Word, I am now saved (Romans 10:9-10). Fill me with Your Holy Spirit for it is He who works in me both to will and to do what pleases You (Philippians 2:13).

Give me a hunger and a thirst for righteousness, and a passion for prayer and Your Word. I also ask that You help me be faithful in my church attendance and readily share my faith with others.

Thank You, Father, for adopting me into Your family (Romans 8:15). In the name of Jesus, I pray. Amen.

I'm Too Busy to Pray

✚ Lord, I'm ready to conquer my prayerlessness. I want my time with You to be my top priority—not just in word but in deed. There are activities I have put before You and in so doing, decided that they are more important. I know that I'm responsible for every activity I have put on my too-busy schedule.

I am not allowing You the time to develop in me the fruit of the Spirit: love, joy, peace, patience, kindness, goodness, faithfulness, gentleness, and self-control (Galatians 5:22-23).

I know that apart from You I can do nothing (John 15:5). Trying to run my life in my own strength is more than I can bear. I want to commit now to a regular prayer time with You because prayer is as important to my spirit as oxygen is to my body. Father, help me to start each morning with just _____ minutes of waiting quietly before You—absorbing Your love, Your wisdom, and Your enabling power for the day. Teach me to pray without ceasing (1 Thessalonians 5:17) by being conscious of Your presence throughout the day. Thank You in advance for a dynamic prayer life that will bring glory to You. In the name of Jesus, I pray. Amen.

I Do Not Read My Bible

✚ Father, please forgive me for my disobedience in not studying Your Word on a regular basis. I know that by not reading my Bible, I make myself defenseless against Satan because Your Word is the sword of the Spirit (Ephesians 6:17). I realize that I could have avoided a lot of my past anxieties, problems, and sins if I had hidden Your Word in my heart and not been so ignorant of Your promises (Psalm 119:11).

Father, I want to be prosperous and have good success. You cautioned that the key to fulfilling this desire is to meditate on Your Word day and night and do all that is written in it (Joshua 1:8). I ask You to please give me a hunger and thirst for Your truth. Help me comprehend the practical application of Your commands and precepts. I know that my intellect is insufficient because spiritual things can only be discerned by the Spirit (1 Corinthians 2:14-15).

Thank You, Father, that even now You are giving me the desire to know You through Your Word. With Your help I will read a passage of Scripture on a daily basis and apply it to my life. In the name of Jesus, I pray. Amen.

Help Me to Fast

✚ Lord, I really desire to fast on a regular basis because exercising this spiritual discipline has many benefits. I have tried and failed many times. My spirit is indeed willing, but my flesh is weak (Matthew 26:41).

I want to sharpen my spiritual sensitivity so I may hear Your voice more clearly and become an effective intercessor for my family, my friends, nations, and all in my circle of concern. You have declared that Your chosen fast will loose the bonds of wickedness, undo the heavy burdens, free the oppressed, and break every yoke of bondage (Isaiah 58:6). I understand that some problems, conditions, and situations will only be eliminated by prayer *and* fasting (Matthew 17:21).

Help me not to fast to be seen or exalted by others because Jesus warned that it would be my only reward. I want to fast Your way, in secret, so You will reward me openly (Matthew 6:16-18).

Lord, help me to start where I am right now in my ability to abstain from food—whether it is fasting until a certain hour of the day, eating one meal a day, abstaining from specific foods for a period of time as Daniel did (Daniel 10:3), or a total fast (except for water) for one to several days. Direct my steps, O Lord, and bring me to full maturity in this area. I will give You all the glory for every miracle and every answered prayer. In the name of Jesus, I pray. Amen.

———□———

I'm Angry with God

Father, Satan is trying to capture my reasoning, weaken my spirit, and turn me against You (Job 15:12-13). Yes, I am angry because You have allowed this situation to happen. You had the power to orchestrate a different outcome in this matter, but You chose not to do so. Notwithstanding, Your Word says that all things work together for my good because I love You and I am called according to Your purpose (Romans 8:28). I suppose my anger is evidence that I do not trust Your wisdom and Your sovereign plan for my life. Forgive me for trying to bring You down to my level of thinking.

How great are Your riches and wisdom and knowledge! How impossible it is for me to understand Your decisions and Your methods! (Romans 11:33-35 TLB). Deliver me from carnally minded thinking because when the Holy Spirit controls my mind, there is life, peace, and grace to accept Your decisions (Romans 8:6).

I receive Your grace to let go of my anger. I repent of my mistrust. I submit totally to Your sovereign plan. In the name of Jesus, I pray. Amen.

I Want to Know Why I'm Here

✠ Father, I'm tired of wandering aimlessly through life pursuing no real purpose. This brings no glory to You. You have created all things, and for Your pleasure I was created (Revelation 4:11). You very deliberately formed me in my mother's womb to serve Your purpose in a unique capacity (Isaiah 49:5). I need Your help to make the path to my destiny clear. I want to stop ignoring or minimizing the gifts and talents You have invested in me and acting as if they are of no significance.

I believe my purpose is fulfilled in service to others so please reveal to me, in a very clear way, how I can serve mankind with everything You have given to me.

I want to do only those things You have destined for me to do and not be distracted by busy-work, wrong priorities, or the desires and demands of others. At the end of my life, I want to be able to say like Jesus, "I brought glory to You here on earth by doing everything You told me to" (John 17:4 TLB). In the name of Jesus, I pray. Amen.

I Have to Make a Decision Now

✠ Father, I need Your guidance and Your wisdom to make the right choice in this very important matter. Your Word says that if I resist being wise in my own eyes, lean not to my own understanding, and acknowledge You in all my ways, You will direct my paths (Proverbs 3:5-7). You promised to instruct me, teach me in the way I should go, and guide me with Your eye (Psalm 32:8).

I want to pursue Your perfect plan for my life. Help me understand that although there may be many plans in my heart, it is Your purpose that will prevail (Proverbs 19:21). Therefore, by the power of Your Holy Spirit, I submit all of my druthers and desires to You now.

Lord, I do not want to make this decision in isolation. Please send godly people across my path who will give me wise input because Your Word says that in the multitude of counselors there is safety (Proverbs 11:14). Help me hear instruction, be wise, and refuse it not (Proverbs 8:33).

For You are my rock and my fortress; therefore, for Your name's sake lead me and guide me (Psalm 31:3). In the name of Jesus, I pray. Amen.

I'm Filled with Pride

✚ Lord, I'm in a spiritual crisis because I have allowed pride to enter my heart. Because of my hard work and man's accolades, I find myself taking personal credit for what You have allowed me to acquire or accomplish. But who makes me different from anyone else? What do I have that I did not receive? And if I did receive it, why do I act as though I did not? (1 Corinthians 4:6-7).

Help me, Lord. I know that pride will prevent me from having a close relationship with You because You resist the proud, but give grace to the humble (James 4:6).

Help me to walk in humility. Your Word says that pride goes before destruction and a haughty spirit before a fall (Proverbs 16:18). I know that pride will bring me low, but those who are humble in spirit will retain honor (Proverbs 29:23).

I am sorry, Lord. I humble myself now. I resist the spirit of pride and command it to flee according to Your Word (James 4:7). In my heart and before men, I will give You all the glory from this day forward. In the name of Jesus, I pray. Amen.

I'm Robbing God

Father, I come before You today, asking forgiveness for robbing You of Your tithes and offerings (Malachi 3:8; Matthew 23:23). I know that all of the money You have allowed me to earn belongs to You and I must pay a required portion back to You. I repent now for being a poor and disobedient steward of Your resources.

I understand that if I obey You by paying my tithes, You will rebuke Satan when he comes to devour my blessings (Malachi 3:11). In addition, You promise to open the windows of heaven and pour out blessings so great that I will not have enough room to take them in (Malachi 3:10).

Lord, help me reject the spirit of fear that keeps me from bringing my entire tithe, ten percent of my income, to the church so the needs of the ministry will be met (Malachi 3:10). I know that You love a cheerful giver (2 Corinthians 9:7). Cause me, therefore, to willingly, cheerfully, and faithfully bring my tithes and offerings. I know that my obedience will insure me against lack. In the name of Jesus, I pray. Amen.

Lying Seems the Only Way Out

✚ Father, I'm in a situation where telling a lie seems to be the best solution to the problem. Even though I have reached this conclusion based upon my natural reasoning, I'm coming to You because Your Word says that You detest lying lips, but You delight in those who are truthful (Proverbs 12:22). Father, I want my actions to delight You; I do not want to engage in any behavior You hate. I want to walk as an upright person guided by integrity (Proverbs 11:3).

Your Word says that truth stands the test of time, and lies are soon exposed (Proverbs 12:19). Give me the courage now to put away all lying and deceitfulness and tell the truth (Ephesians 4:25).

I leave the consequences of telling the truth to You, knowing You will work everything out for my good (Romans 8:28). I know that this will be far better than the consequences of lying because Your Word says that he who works deceit shall not dwell within Your house; he who tells lies shall not continue in Your presence (Psalm 101:7). Give me the courage to speak the truth now. In the name of Jesus, I pray. Amen.

My Loved One Needs Salvation

✚ Father, my heart is burdened for _____
because he/she has not accepted Jesus as his/her
personal Savior. He/she is trying to live on this earth
without a relationship with You. I can't stand the thought
of him/her spending eternity in hell. I know that You
have been long-suffering toward him/her because You
are not willing that any should perish, but all should come
to repentance (2 Peter 3:9). Notwithstanding, You said
that even though all souls belong to You, the soul that
practices sin shall die (Ezekiel 18:20) and be eternally
separated from You.

O Lord, please send someone across _____'s
path to minister salvation to him/her. You said that no
man can come to Jesus unless You draw him (John 6:44).
Prepare his/her heart now; do not let him/her resist the
courting by Your Spirit.

I take authority over the stronghold of sin captivating
_____'s mind. Let him/her find no comfort, joy,
or fulfillment in his/her life of rebellion.

Help me to let my light shine before him/her so he/she
will see the joy, peace, and other benefits of salvation. I
pray You fill _____ with the knowledge of Your will
through all spiritual wisdom and understanding, and
he/she may live a life worthy of You and may please You
in every way—bearing fruit in every good work, growing
in the knowledge of You (Colossians 1:9-10). In the name
of Jesus, I pray. Amen.

Part 2

Prayers for Physical Crises

I'm in Physical Danger

Lord, You are my hiding place; You protect me from trouble (Psalm 32:7). Even when I walk through the dark valley of death, I will not be afraid because You are close beside me. Your rod and Your staff protect and comfort me (Psalm 23:4).

Thank You, Lord, for being my light and my salvation. Why should I be afraid? You protect me from danger—so why should I tremble? (Psalm 27:1,3).

Lord, let this situation be a reminder that I need to walk uprightly before You faithfully so I can confidently claim Your promises of protection, because You rescue the godly from danger, but You let the wicked fall into trouble (Proverbs 11:8).

I rest in the assurance no harm will befall me; no disaster will come near me for You have commanded Your angels to guard me in all my ways (Psalm 91:10-11).

Thank You for Your faithfulness to me. In the name of Jesus, I pray. Amen.

I Have a Life-Threatening Illness

✚ Father, the enemy has come to steal my life because that is what he does: steals, kills, and destroys. But I trust in Your Word which says You have come that I may have life, and have it to the full (John 10:10). Even though the doctor's report is negative, I know that You have the last word regarding my life. You saw me before I was born. Every day of my life was recorded in Your book. Every moment was laid out before a single day had passed (Psalm 139:16).

Forgive me, Father, for any door I may have opened for this sickness by not being a good steward of my health. Surround me with Your tender mercies so I may live (Psalm 119:77). Raise me up as a testimony of Your great healing power. You are the same miracle working God yesterday, and today, and forever (Hebrews 13:8).

I take authority over every malfunctioning part of my body. I command each one to be made whole. I decree that I will not die before my appointed time, but will live to tell what You have done (Psalm 118:17). Therefore, I say on the authority of Your Word, that with the stripes of Jesus, I am healed! (Isaiah 53:5). In the name of Jesus, I pray. Amen.

My Pain Won't Go Away

Lord, I'm in pain and You only are my refuge, my strength, and a very present help in times of trouble (Psalm 46:1). Your Word says that many are the afflictions of the righteous, but You deliver him out of them all (Psalm 34:19). Look upon my affliction and my pain, and forgive all my sins (Psalm 25:18). Send relief now, Lord. Whether You choose medicine or a miracle, I will forever acknowledge You as the Source of my healing.

Help me shift my focus from my pain to Your promises because they revive me and comfort me (Psalm 119:50). Heal me, O Lord, and I will be healed; save me and I will be saved for You are the one who deserves my praise (Jeremiah 17:14).

Let, I pray, Your merciful kindness be for my comfort, according to Your Word (Psalm 119:76). On the authority of Your Word, I declare that Your anointing is driving the pain out of my body now! In the name of Jesus, I pray. Amen.

My Appetite Is Out of Control

Lord, I have allowed food to take center stage in my life, and I'm in trouble. I know that it displeases You when I am out of control like this. Your Word declares that every person who strives for the mastery must be temperate in all things (1 Corinthians 9:25). I repent for not allowing the Holy Spirit to produce the fruit of temperance in my life (Galatians 5:22-23). Your Word says that the righteous eats to the satisfying of his soul, but the belly of the wicked shall want (Proverbs 13:25). Teach me how to eat until satisfied and not to stuff myself. Search my heart and shine the light on whatever emotional issue is eating me and causing me to consume excessive amounts of food (Psalm 139:23-24). Show me how to deal with the problem apart from food. Help me become nutritionally smart. I do not want my body to be destroyed for lack of knowledge (Hosea 4:6). Cause me to desire only those foods that will nourish my body.

I submit my appetite to Your Spirit. Therefore, whether I eat or drink or whatever I do, help me do it all for Your glory (1 Corinthians 10:31). In the name of Jesus, I pray. Amen.

I Need to Start Exercising Now

Lord, I know my body is the temple of the Holy Spirit, and it is not my own (1 Corinthians 6:19). I confess that I have failed in my stewardship of this area by not exercising regularly. Your Word says that I was bought by Jesus at a great price, and I should glorify You in my body and in my spirit because they both belong to You (1 Corinthians 6:20).

Lord, I know that You want my body and my soul to be equally healthy (3 John 1:2). Help me bring my body into subjection to my spirit and make it my slave (1 Corinthians 9:27). I do not want to open the door for Satan to come in and attack my body through weak limbs, poor blood circulation, obesity, lethargy, or other maladies. As I begin to exercise, help me keep the right perspective on the purpose of a fit body and not be driven by the world's standards of trying to entice the opposite sex.

I need You, Father, to work in me both to will and to do Your good pleasure (Philippians 2:13). I can't do it in my own strength; apart from You I can do nothing (John 15:5). By Your grace I will be holy and fit! In the name of Jesus, I pray. Amen.

I'm Physically or Mentally Fatigued

✚ Lord, I am so exhausted. Nevertheless, I find comfort and refuge in Jesus' invitation to come to Him for rest when we are overburdened with heavy responsibilities (Matthew 11:28). I am indeed overloaded. I long to enter into that special rest that waits for the people of God (Hebrews 4:9-11).

Teach me how to make the most of my time so I will prioritize and manage my day with wisdom (Psalm 90:12). I'm tired of being the daily victim of the urgent versus what's really important. Most of all, let me not forget to acknowledge You and submit my schedule to You before I commit to a single activity. Give me the courage to say no when it is appropriate and wise to do so. Let me not allow worldly values to drive me to acquire things or pursue vain goals that keep me from getting proper rest. Teach me how to wait in Your presence. I stand on Your Word, trusting You will renew my strength like that of the eagle and cause me to soar to new heights (Isaiah 40:31). In the name of Jesus, I pray. Amen.

I Can't Sleep

Father, I thank You for Your promise to give rest to Your loved ones (Psalm 127:2). I ask You to shine Your light on the root cause of my sleeplessness. Whatever anxieties are preventing me from entering into a state of restorative slumber, I cast them all on You now as You have instructed for You care for me (1 Peter 5:7).

Calm my racing mind. Help me be still and know that You are God (Psalm 46:10). I submit to Your command to refrain from worrying about anything and pray about everything. I bring my needs to You and thank You for all You have done. Your Word assures me that as I do this, I will experience Your peace, which is far more wonderful than the human mind can understand. Your peace will guard my heart and my mind (Philippians 4:6-7).

By faith, I will lie down without fear or anxiety, and I will enjoy pleasant dreams (Proverbs 3:24). Yes, I will lie down in peace and sleep because You alone, O Lord, will keep me safe (Psalms 4:8). In the name of Jesus, I pray. Amen.

My Death Is Imminent

✝ Father, I know my departure from this earth is just a matter of time. I may not have done everything You told me to do; nevertheless, I ask that You extend mercy to me as You did the thief who died on the cross alongside Jesus (Luke 23:42-43). Thank You for the salvation of my soul through Christ's crucifixion, burial, and resurrection.

Father, I find comfort in knowing there will be no more death, or sorrow, or crying, or pain in the world to come (Revelation 21:4). Because I have asked You to be my Lord and Savior, I look forward to that blessed day without fear.

Father, do not let my dying be in vain. Rather, use my death to draw people to You. Let this be a time when they reflect on their own mortality and commit to pursuing Your purpose for their lives.

Finally I pray that before heaven's doors close, my entire family will say yes to Your will for their lives and that we will all rejoice around Your throne together. In the name of Jesus, I pray. Amen.

■ Part 3

Prayers for Marriage Crises

I've Fallen Out of Love with My Mate

✚ Father, my affections for my spouse are at an all-time low. I know that Your Word says that unfailing love is patient, kind, humble, not rude, not self-seeking, not easily angered, and keeps no record of wrongs (1 Corinthians 13:4-5). I confess that I have kept records of all offenses and now I have no patience with his/her shortcomings. Forgive me, Father, for my spiritual immaturity. I ask You to come into my heart and love my spouse through me. Help me release every offense. I want my marriage to be a model of how Christ loved the church and gave Himself for it.

Lord, work in us both to will and to do Your good pleasure (Philippians 2:13). Heal our marriage for Your glory. Guide us as we follow the pattern in Your Word for recapturing lost love: remembering the things we used to do, repenting of our failings, and rekindling the fire we had in the beginning (Revelation 2:5). Only You can change a person's heart; therefore, I submit my heart and my emotions to You now to turn as You will (Proverbs 21:1). In the name of Jesus, I pray. Amen.

I Do Not Want to Submit to My Husband

✠ Lord, I know that Your Word says that I must submit to my husband in everything (as long as he is not requiring me to sin or break the law) for this is Your divine order (Ephesians 5:22-24); however, I'm having trouble doing so. Whether my attitude is attributable to my need to control or to my opinion that I'm more qualified to lead in certain areas, I do not want to be in rebellion because it is as bad as the sin of witchcraft, and stubbornness is as bad as worshiping idols (1 Samuel 15:23).

So, Father, help me humble myself and submit to my husband—even when I do not feel like doing so. Make me a good helper. Give him the wisdom, courage, and knowledge to direct our household in a God-honoring way. Teach me how to genuinely support his decisions and not second-guess him. Help me, Lord, to discipline my tongue so my words encourage and build him up (Ephesians 4:29) rather than diminish him. By Your grace I will be a wise woman who builds her house, rather than the foolish one who tears it down with her own hands (Proverbs 14:1). In the name of Jesus, I pray. Amen.

I'm Tired of Wearing the Pants

✚ Father, I repent for taking my husband's place as the head of our household. The more authority I have usurped from him, the more he has regressed in his leadership role. I know that this is not Your divine order for our marriage. I understand the husband is the head of the wife, even as Christ is the head of the church (Ephesians 5:23). However, being an independent, strong-willed woman is what I became in order to survive life's negative experiences.

I ask You to give me the courage to repent to my husband for causing him to default on his God-given responsibilities. I sincerely desire to hand the reins back to him. I rebuke the fear that he will make a mess of things. My eyes are on You to cause him to do exceedingly abundantly above all I ask or think, according to Your power that works in him (Ephesians 3:20).

Show me specific ways day by day to get back into my rightful place. Change my controlling attitude. Help me release my emotional baggage so my husband can become the provider and protector You have called him to be. In the name of Jesus, I pray. Amen.

*I Need to Get Away from My Abusive Husband**

✝ Father, I am tired of suffering abuse at the hands of my husband. I ask that You deliver me now from the faulty thinking, hopeful fantasies, denial, or the fears that have kept me in this situation.

Your Word says that my husband should love me as he does his own body and care for me just as Christ cares for the church and gave Himself for it (Ephesians 5:28). I realize that he does not love me because love does not hurt anyone (Romans 13:10).

Whether his problem stems from a generational curse of spousal abuse, a chemical imbalance in his brain, or any other cause, I ask that You deliver him now. Send someone across his path who will show him the way out of his bondage. Give me the wisdom to protect myself from his physical or verbal abuse because my body and my mind are Your temple and should not be dishonored in this way (1 Corinthians 6:19).

Give me the courage to remove myself from this abusive environment. I need a place of refuge and support. I stand on Your Word that says You will supply every need I have according to Your great riches in glory (Philippians 4:19). In the name of Jesus, I pray. Amen.

*Can be modified to pray for an abusive wife.

My In-Laws Are Ruining My Marriage

✚ Thank You, Lord, for my spouse. I know that in Your design for marriage, spouses must leave their parents and cleave to their mates in order for them to become one (Genesis 2:24). I need Your help now because my in-laws are a threat to our unity. I'm asking that You give my spouse the courage to be strong in setting boundaries with his/her parents or other meddling relatives. Help him/her overcome the fear of being rejected or judged negatively for putting them in their place. Cause him/her to see that he/she is the one who teaches them how to interact with us by how much interference he/she tolerates.

Let Your Word be our guidebook for everything because we cannot walk together unless we are in agreement on the direction in which we are going (Amos 3:3). Lord, should it become necessary for me to speak to my in-laws directly, give me the tongue of the learned to be gracious and direct in speaking the right words at the right time (Isaiah 50:4) so there will be no permanent damage to our marriage or our relationship with the in-laws.

Thank You in advance for going ahead of us in this matter and making their hearts receptive to our input. In the name of Jesus, I pray. Amen.

We Want to Have a Child

O Lord, we long to have a child of our own. We are frustrated with all of the futile efforts we have made to fulfill this desire. We turn to You as our only hope because all life begins with You. We ask that You grant us the privilege of bringing a child into this world to rear and nurture in your admonition (Ephesians 6:4). Please remove every hindrance and obstacle to our conception.

We stand in faith that You will grant our petition just as You did when Hannah cried out to You for a child (1 Samuel 1:10-17); nevertheless, if in Your infinite wisdom, You have looked into the future and, for whatever reason, determined it is not Your will for us to be the natural father and mother of a child, then we ask that You give us the grace to accept Your decision. Show us the next step to take. Help us exalt Your will above our own desires.

Give us peace as we submit to Your timing and Your sovereign plan now. In the name of Jesus, I pray. Amen.

I've Just Had a Miscarriage

✚ O God, my husband and I are so disappointed because my pregnancy has ended this way. We know that You are the giver of life and You had a divine purpose in allowing me to conceive. I resist any attempt to bring You down to my level of understanding for Your wisdom and knowledge are unsearchable, and Your ways, decisions, and methods are past finding out (Romans 11:33-34).

We stand on the truths found in Your Word. We know that when You form a life in the womb, You have already decided what purpose it will serve (Isaiah 49:5). At conception, You determined the number of days this child would live and wrote them in Your book (Psalm 139:16). We are assured that when You purpose something, no one can thwart or annul Your plans (Isaiah 14:27). So, Lord, help us no longer refer to this situation as a "mis-carriage" or pregnancy failure, but as an "in-womb life completion."

Of course we had great plans for this child's future; however, in Proverbs 19:21 (NIV) Your Word declares, "Many are the plans in a man's heart, but it is the LORD's purpose that prevails." Comfort us, Father, so we can comfort others who may experience this hurt (2 Corinthians 1:4). Be glorified in our response as we model faith, hope, and trust in You. In the name of Jesus, I pray. Amen.

My Spouse Wants a Divorce

✝ Father, You said that You hate divorce (Malachi 2:16). I do not desire, nor have I initiated, such action, but my spouse's wishes are out of my hands. Even though the situation looks hopeless, I know that You are the God of all flesh and nothing is too hard for You (Jeremiah 32:17). Therefore, Father, I stand in faith for the restoration of my marriage. Your Word declares that even the heart of the king is in Your hands and You can turn it any way You please (Proverbs 21:1); even so, Lord, I ask that You turn my spouse's heart back to me.

Take the scales from my eyes; show me where I have erred and contributed to his/her wanting to divorce me. I know that You can strengthen me to make the necessary changes in my behavior (Philippians 4:13).

I resist all anxiety regarding any aspect of my future because You promised never to leave me nor forsake me (Hebrews 13:5). Thank You for Your faithfulness to me. I now receive Your peace, which passes my understanding (Philippians 4:6-7). In the name of Jesus, I pray. Amen.

My Spouse Has Been Unfaithful

Father, my spouse has violated our marriage vows, which You said should be honored and the marriage bed kept pure (Hebrews 13:4). I am so hurt. Help me resist the temptation to redress this wrong because You said You will judge the adulterer and all the sexually immoral (Hebrews 13:4).

Give me the desire to forgive him/her for I am reminded that while I was yet a sinner, You showed Your love by sending Jesus to die for me (Romans 5:8). I need You to do a special work in my heart now and give me the strength to exercise agape love and true forgiveness. I repent for any role I played that may have encouraged his/her actions. Reveal it to me now and please do not let guilt over it torment me.

Lord, according to Your Word, adultery is legitimate grounds for divorce (Matthew 19:9); however, if this is not Your will, give me the grace to overcome the hurt of this betrayal. Teach me how to trust again and not become bitter. Give my spouse the wisdom to avoid future situations that make it easy to fulfill the lust of the flesh (Romans 13:14). Take this situation Satan meant for bad and turn it into a testimony for Your glory. I submit to Your sovereign will in this matter. In the name of Jesus, I pray. Amen.

I'm Having an Emotional Affair

✝ Father, I confess that I am having an emotional affair. I know that cleaving to another in this way is a gross violation of my marriage vows (Matthew 19:5-6). This person is fulfilling an emotional need I have; one my spouse is unaware of or unwilling to meet. I know that this does not justify my behavior.

I realize I'm opening the door for full-blown sexual infidelity. Your Word says that a prudent person foresees the danger and takes refuge, but the simple keep going and suffer for it (Proverbs 27:12). I do not want to keep being foolish, nor do I want to suffer the loss of my marriage. I need to terminate this harmful relationship now. Help me to immediately stop the secret e-mails, the phone calls, the inappropriate compliments, or any other actions that keep this immoral fire burning.

Forgive me for being ignorant of Satan's schemes and devices and falling into his trap (2 Corinthians 2:11). Teach me and my spouse how to effectively communicate our needs to each other and take steps to fulfill them within the bounds of our marriage. In the name of Jesus, I pray. Amen.

My Spouse and I Rarely Have Sex

✚ Lord, contrary to Your will, sex is not an integral part of our marriage relationship. I'm coming to You for wisdom on how to get this area back on track. I know Your Word says the husband should not deprive his wife of sexual intimacy, which is her right as a married woman. Nor should the wife deprive her husband of sexual relations—except when they agree to fast and pray for a set period of time (1 Corinthians 7:3-5).

Shine the light on the root cause of the problem so we can determine whether it is due to emotional, medical, or relationship factors, or a combination of them. Help us discuss this issue honestly and openly, without blame, ridicule, or harsh words. Let us be willing to get professional help if necessary. I do not want frustration and resentment to get a foothold in our relationship. Help us realize that we make ourselves vulnerable to Satan's attack by our failure to become one flesh on a regular basis (1 Corinthians 7:5). Show each of us creative ways to reignite our passion and bring sexual fulfillment to our marriage. In the name of Jesus, I pray. Amen.

My Spouse Is Insanely Jealous

✚ Father, I am fed up with my jealous, mistrustful spouse. Your Word says that jealousy is as cruel as the grave, and its flames are flames of fire (Song of Solomon 8:6). Yes, the flames of his/her jealousy are consuming our marriage. He/she has no peace as he/she tries to control my every move. He/she is tormented with the fear of being displaced. Father, please draw him/her into a close relationship with You because Your perfect love casts out fear, and fear involves torment. Help him/her see the person who fears has not been made perfect in Your love (1 John 4:18).

Show me how I may be contributing to his/her insecurity by poorly communicating my whereabouts, minimizing his/her concern, flirting with the opposite sex, or any other actions. Give me the grace and love to be long-suffering and supportive (1 Corinthians 13:4). Let him/her find the help he/she needs to deal with the events of his/her past that gave birth to his/her fear of being abandoned. I pray that he/she will learn to trust You to the point he/she will believe Your promise to guard and secure whatever You have given to him/her (Psalm 16:5). Thank You in advance for his/her deliverance now. In the name of Jesus, I pray. Amen.

My Spouse Is Financially Irresponsible

✚ Lord, my spouse's irresponsible behavior is threatening the financial stability of our marriage. I do not want Satan to use our different attitudes about money to destroy our relationship. I ask that You fill the emptiness that drives his/her behavior. Give me the wisdom to pray for, encourage, and build him/her up (1 Thessalonians 5:11) rather than resorting to nagging, name-calling, or putdowns because of his/her apparent lack of good financial judgment. Cause him/her to see the error of his/her ways. Give him/her the desire to handle the money You provide according to biblical principles of good stewardship.

Lord, search my heart and show me where my mindset regarding our finances may be too conservative and, thus, hindering us from experiencing the abundant life Jesus came to give (John 10:10). Show us both how to strike a balance between spending for enjoyment today and saving for the future. Deliver us from the emotional baggage that has shaped our views about the purpose and priority of our finances. Let us forsake and forget these destructive attitudes and look forward to what lies ahead in our relationship (Philippians 3:13). Help us reach one accord in our priorities for Your Word says two cannot walk together unless they are in agreement (Amos 3:3).

Thank You in advance for raising us up to be an example and testimony of a couple walking in financial intimacy and victory. In the name of Jesus, I pray. Amen.

Part 4

Prayers for Children
and Relatives in Crisis

A Loved One Needs Protection

✚ Father, in my distress I cry unto You and You hear me (Psalm 120:1). I come to You on behalf of _____ who needs Your protection now. What a comfort to know that we are never away from Your presence (Psalm 139:7). I stand on Your Word and believe when _____ goes through deep waters and great trouble, You will be with him/her. When he/she goes through rivers of difficulty, he/she will not drown! When he/she walks through the fire of oppression, he/she will not be consumed (Isaiah 43:2).

I thank You for sending Your angels now to protect _____ in all his/her ways (Psalm 91:11). I thank You because Your plans for _____ are for good and not for disaster, to give him/her a future and a hope (Jeremiah 29:11).

I reject every anxious or doubtful thought. I cast all my care regarding this situation upon You because You care for _____ (1 Peter 5:7). Thank You for Your faithfulness in strengthening and protecting _____ from the works of Satan (2 Thessalonians 3:3). I praise You in advance for the good report I will receive regarding his/her safety and deliverance from this threatening situation. In the name of Jesus, I pray. Amen.

Strife Is Tearing My Family Apart

O Lord, strife is wreaking havoc in our family. Your Word says that those who sow discord are an abomination to You (Proverbs 6:16,19). I ask You to touch the hearts of every contentious family member and draw them closer to You. You said that those who are peacemakers are blessed and shall be called Your children (Matthew 5:9). Father, I commit myself to be the peacemaker in this situation.

Deliver my family from selfishness, pride, and hatred. Give us the kind of love that covers all sins and shortcomings (Proverbs 10:12). Help us know when a disagreement is about to open a floodgate and drop the matter before the dispute gets out of control (Proverbs 17:14). Your Word says that avoiding a fight is a mark of honor, and only fools insist on quarreling (Proverbs 20:3). Silence the fools, Father.

I take authority over every divisive spirit. I ask You to help my family begin to pursue the things which make for peace and the things by which we may edify one another (Romans 14:19). In the name of Jesus, I pray. Amen.

I'm Guilty of Child Abuse

Father, I know that children are special to You because Jesus rebuked His disciples for trying to push the children aside when their parents brought them to Him (Mark 10:13). Just as He took the little children in His arms, touched them, and blessed them (Mark 10:16), help me to interact with my child in a way that will bless, rather than curse, him/her. Deliver me from the rage that would cause me to physically or verbally abuse him/her or any other child. Help me submit myself to the Holy Spirit and allow Him to work the fruit of love, patience, gentleness, and long-suffering in me (Galatians 5:22).

Your Word says that if I spare the rod, I hate and will spoil my child, but if I love him/her, I will be careful to discipline him/her (Proverbs 13:24). Teach me, Father, how to discipline my child with wisdom because I realize that I also do him/her great harm if I spare him/her the rod of correction.

Forgive me for the parenting mistakes I have made in the past. Continue to remind me, Father, children are a heritage from You and the fruit of the womb is a reward (Psalms 127:3). I am depending on You to make me the parent You have called me to be. In the name of Jesus, I pray. Amen.

My Child Is Out of Control

Father, my child's behavior is out of control. I realize that he/she is a product of my parenting. Forgive me for defaulting on Your mandate to raise him/her with the discipline and instruction approved by You (Ephesians 6:4). I'm ready to parent Your way now.

I need You, Father, to teach me how to set boundaries with appropriate and consistent consequences. Your Word says that a youngster's heart is filled with foolishness, but discipline will drive it away (Proverbs 22:15). Help me, Lord, overcome the fear of my child rejecting me when I make an unpopular, but wise decision. I know that this insecurity comes from Satan because You have not given me the spirit of fear, but of power, and of love, and of a sound mind (2 Timothy 1:7).

Let me have appropriate expectations of my child so I will not provoke or frustrate him/her (Colossians 3:21). By faith, I decree that my child will be taught of the Lord and his/her peace will be great (Isaiah 54:13). Thank You in advance for being glorified in his/her life. In the name of Jesus, I pray. Amen.

My Daughter Is Pregnant Out of Wedlock

Father, I am so disappointed because my daughter is pregnant out of wedlock. Even though You are the giver of all life, I know that this is not the ideal circumstance under which a child should be born. You said that fornication is wrong and my daughter should have fled from her youthful lusts (2 Timothy 2:22). Nevertheless, You have a sovereign purpose in allowing her to conceive. According to Your Word, all the days ordained for this child, though he/she is yet unborn, have already been written in Your book (Psalm 139:16).

Forgive me for any failure on my part that contributed to this situation. Help me be a wise parent, giving her the necessary support, but not to the extent it will enable her to repeat this experience. Guide me as I counsel her in her decision to keep the baby or to release him/her for adoption. I also pray that the baby's father will play an integral role in making the decision that will affect this child's destiny. I now put away all bitterness, rage, and anger I might feel toward the baby's father (Ephesians 4:31).

I decree by faith that this child will bring glory and honor to Your name as he/she fulfills his/her purpose for being born. In the name of Jesus, I pray. Amen.

My Son or Daughter Is Gay

✝ Lord, according to Your Word, homosexuality is detestable in Your sight (Leviticus 20:13). I pray You open the eyes of my son/daughter's understanding so he/she may know the hope to which You have called him/her (Ephesians 1:18).

Father, let me demonstrate an attitude of compassion and encouragement rather than condemnation. I need Your grace to show Your unconditional love. Help me refrain from exalting the sin of homosexuality above any other moral failing for Your Word says that all unrighteousness is sin (1 John 5:17). Please extend Your mercy now, Father. Do not turn my child over to a reprobate or debased mind as You did the Gentiles who engaged in same-sex intercourse (Romans 1:28).

I bind every demonic spirit that is influencing my son's/daughter's emotions and perverting his/her affections (Matthew 18:18). I decree that my child will fully embrace the gender You created him/her to be (Genesis 1:27). I also decree that he/she is being transformed now by the renewing of his/her mind and he/she will prove Your good, acceptable, and perfect will (Romans 12:2). In the name of Jesus, I pray. Amen.

I'm Tired of My Freeloading Son or Daughter

Lord, I confess that I have enabled my adult child to become irresponsible. I repent of my failure now. Your Word declares that every person must bear responsibility for their own behavior (Galatians 6:5). Forgive me for every time I rescued him/her with my safety net and did not allow him/her to reap the consequences of his/her unwise choices. Help me acknowledge and forsake my own guilt, fears, emotional vacuums, or erroneous beliefs that caused me to deal with him/her this way (Psalm 51:6). I realize my child is now an adult and I should have worked myself out of the job of parenting him/her long ago.

I am ready to establish appropriate boundaries now, and I need You to give me the courage to do so. I believe that as I do my part, my child will begin to model the example of apostle Paul who was never lazy when he stayed in people's homes, never accepted food without paying for it, and worked hard day and night so he would not be a burden to anyone (2 Thessalonians 3:7-8). I declare by faith that my child will develop into an emotionally, financially, and spiritually mature adult whose life will bring honor and glory to You. In the name of Jesus, I pray. Amen.

I'm Weary of Caring for My Elderly Parent

✝ Lord, I thank You for my parent, whom You chose to bring me into this world. Surely I could never repay him/her for all the sacrifices he/she has made for me during his/her lifetime. Indeed, Your Word says that it pleases You very much when children take the responsibility to support needy parents, for kindness should begin at home (1 Timothy 5:4).

Father, You commanded children to honor their parents, and as a result You would grant them a long life (Ephesians 6:2-3). I want to continue honoring my parent by giving him/her the best of care. Nevertheless, Father, I am physically and emotionally spent with the enormity of this responsibility.

Help me spend time waiting in Your presence so You will renew my strength (Isaiah 40:31). Show me a more effective way to fulfill my duties as a caregiver or conservator. Give me the wisdom to get proper rest and relief so Satan will not use my fatigue to cause me to become impatient and unloving toward my parent.

Thank You for being my heavenly parent who is with me always and who will never leave nor forsake me (Hebrews 13:5). In the name of Jesus, I pray. Amen.

■ Part 5

Prayers for Relationship Crises

I Want to Be Married Now

✚ Father, Your Word says that if I delight myself in You, You will give me the desires of my heart (Psalm 37:4). I desire a Spirit-filled soul mate. I want my conduct to honor You while I wait for Your perfect choice and timing. Give me the strength, by the power of the Holy Spirit, to mortify the deeds of my body (Romans 8:13) and avoid fornication because Your Word declares that every man should have his own wife, and each woman her own husband (1 Corinthians 7:2).

Show me ways to practice Your kind of love even now while I am single. Help me be patient, kind, not proud, not rude, not self-seeking, not easily angered, keeping no record of wrongs, not delighting in evil, but rejoicing with the truth (1 Corinthians 13:4-6).

Search me, Father, and know my heart. Point out anything in me that offends You (Psalm 139:23-24). Help me forsake destructive habits, ungodly mindsets, emotional baggage, and all behavior that will threaten the happiness and unity of my marriage.

Let me not expect my mate to fulfill me in ways only You can. Teach me how to feel complete and satisfied with You and You alone. Help me not become weary with the wait for I know in due season You will bring about my marriage (Galatians 6:9). In the name of Jesus, I pray. Amen.

I'm in Love with Mr. or Miss Wrong

✚ Father, I know in my heart that _____ is not
the person You have chosen to be my life partner.
However, I desire to be with him/her anyway. I know that
You can redirect my emotions because even a king's heart
is in Your hands, and You direct it like a watercourse
wherever You please (Proverbs 21:1). Lord, I ask that You
break the emotional bond between me and _____
and destroy this unequal yoke.

I want to love only the person You have chosen for
me. Help me take a close look at my values and insecu-
rities and reject whatever causes me to be drawn to the
wrong type of person. I do not want to be shallow or use
worldly criteria in evaluating my potential mate. Cause
me to heed the warning signs You are trying to show me
and not rationalize them away.

Give me a desire to seek first Your kingdom and Your
righteousness so everything else I need will be added to
me (Matthew 6:33). Teach me how to wait patiently for
You because You will bring to pass in Your due season
everything I need (Psalm 37:7). In the name of Jesus, I
pray. Amen.

I'm Tempted to Have
Sex Outside of Marriage

✚ Lord, I am tempted to engage in sex outside of the bonds of marriage. You have warned me against making provisions to fulfill the lust of my flesh by creating an environment that is conducive to indulging such passions (Romans 13:14). Yes, I know that my body is the temple of the Holy Spirit and it belongs to You. I sincerely desire to honor You with my body (1 Corinthians 6:19-20).

Teach me how to put to death the sinful, earthly things lurking within me and have nothing to do with sexual sin, impurity, or lust (Colossians 3:5).

I stand on Your Word that declares You are faithful, You will not allow me to be tempted beyond my capacity to resist, and with every temptation, You will also make a way of escape so that I will not give in (1 Corinthians 10:13). I thank You now for the strength to pursue the way of escape. By faith I will consider myself dead to sexual sin and able to live for Your glory (Romans 6:11) as I wait for You to bring me together with my chosen life's partner. In the name of Jesus, I pray. Amen.

Someone Has Betrayed My Trust

✚ O God, I trusted _____ and he/she has betrayed my confidence. I feel hurt, violated, saddened, and angry by his/her deceptive behavior.

I know that Jesus suffered the ultimate betrayal at the hands of Judas Iscariot (John 6:71), yet He did not let it stop Him from loving others and pursuing His purpose. Help me respond likewise. Don't let this betrayal cause me to alienate or avoid others nor suspect everyone of insincere motives. I refuse to allow a root of bitterness to spring up and defile me or other people in my circle of interaction (Hebrews 12:15). Remove from me any desire to avenge this wrong by rendering evil for evil (1 Thessalonians 5:15).

Help me be more discerning and use greater wisdom in my relationships. In the total scheme of my life, You have a good purpose for allowing this to happen (Romans 8:28). I submit to Your sovereign agenda.

Lord, it is You who works in me to will and to do of Your good pleasure (Philippians 2:13). Please give me the desire and the strength to release _____ from this offense and extend complete forgiveness. In the name of Jesus, I pray. Amen.

I Need to Overcome Rejection

✚ Father, You know the hurt that I feel because _____ has rejected me. Despite my emotional pain, help me take an honest look at the aspects of my behavior that may have contributed to this rejection. You want me to be truthful in my innermost being (Psalm 51:6) so please help me accept the appropriate level of personal responsibility in this situation. Notwithstanding, let me also understand sometimes man's rejection could very well be Your protection from a bigger hurt in the future. I trust every relationship to You, Father.

I take my shield of faith and quench this fiery dart of rejection (Ephesians 6:16). It shall not pierce my emotions. I will not respond to this rejection with bitterness, self-pity, or any other negative emotion that will mar my future. I will respond in the same manner as my Savior, who was despised, rejected, and well acquainted with grief (Isaiah 53:3), yet He forgave His offenders for He knew that His rejection served a higher purpose.

Give me the wisdom to perceive that my "merchandise is good" (Proverbs 31:18); that I still bring something of value to the table in any relationship. I thank You, Father, for adopting me into Your family and accepting me in the Beloved (Ephesians 1:6). In the name of Jesus, I pray. Amen.

I've Been Falsely Accused

✝ Father, I have been falsely accused. I know the lie originated with Satan because he is the father of lies (John 8:44). I also know that You have the power to vindicate me and silence the lying lips (Psalm 31:18). Let me not be put to shame, O Lord, for I cry out to You. Let the wicked be put to shame and let their lying lips be silenced for speaking against me (Psalm 31:17-18). Cause their deceitful words to lose their impact and find no fertile ground.

I stand on Your promise that declares no weapon formed against me will succeed, and You will condemn every tongue that rises against me. Yes, being vindicated by You is one of the fringe benefits I enjoy as Your servant (Isaiah 54:17).

Lord, let me never be a false witness for I know that I will not go unpunished (Proverbs 19:9). Your Word says that no one who practices deceit will dwell in Your house; no one who speaks falsely will stand in Your presence (Psalm 101:7). I want to stand with clean hands and a pure heart before You. Like Jesus when He was falsely accused, I refuse to retaliate. I put the situation in Your hands completely. Vindicate me, Father. In the name of Jesus, I pray. Amen.

I'm Offended

✚ Lord, I am upset and offended by _____'s words or actions. Your Word says, "A man's wisdom gives him patience; it is to his glory to overlook an offense" (Proverbs 19:11 NIV). However, it also says, "If thy brother shall trespass against thee, go and tell him his fault between thee and him alone" (Matthew 18:15 KJV).

I need You to help me determine whether to overlook or confront this situation. Either way my most urgent request is that You help me forgive quickly. Do not let me fall into Satan's trap of offense by developing a root of bitterness against _____ (Hebrews 12:15-16).

Help me give _____ the benefit of the doubt because he/she may not be aware of how his/her words affected me. Should You lead me to confront him/her rather than overlooking this offense, give me Your words to speak because the words that come forth from Your mouth do not return to You void. They accomplish Your purpose and prosper where You send them (Isaiah 55:11). Let my offender be receptive to my input and let us walk in harmony as a result.

Teach me how to become so secure in my relationship with You that man's words will not pierce my mind or my emotions. In the name of Jesus, I pray. Amen.

I Shouldn't Have Said That

✚ Lord, that little unruly member of my body has gotten me into trouble again. Your Word says that no one can tame the tongue and it is an uncontrollable evil, full of deadly poison. Sometimes I use it to praise You and sometimes I use it to hurt those who have been made in Your image (James 3:7-10). Forgive me, Lord, for not allowing You to control my tongue. Teach me how to stop, think, and pray before I speak. Help me realize that even though no *man* can tame the tongue, the things that are impossible with men are possible with You (Luke 18:27). I know that negative words never die but lodge as shrapnel in the mind of the hearer. Notwithstanding, You have the power to cancel the damaging effects of the unwise words I have spoken. Let me be quick to offer a sincere, heartfelt apology.

Because my words are a verbalization of my thoughts, I submit my thought life to You, Father. Help me dwell on whatever things are true, honest, just, pure, lovely, and of a good report (Philippians 4:8). In so doing, I know that the words of my mouth and the meditation of my heart will be acceptable in Your sight (Psalm 19:14). In the name of Jesus, I pray. Amen.

Gossip Is Getting a Stronghold in My Life

Lord, engaging in conversation about someone's personal affairs is becoming such an enticement for me. Show me what is missing in my life and causes me to be so interested or find such delight in discussing someone's failings, weaknesses, or private matters. Your Word warns that I must give an account on judgment day of every idle word I speak, and that the words I say now will determine my fate then—either I will be justified by them or I will be condemned (Matthew 12:36-37).

Help me avoid people who talk too much, tell secrets, and betray the confidences of others (Proverbs 20:19) because bad company corrupts good character (1 Corinthians 15:33).

Let me not cloak gossip under the guise of a prayer request when in fact I am just using it to spread rumors about someone's private affairs and get attention. I do not want to reap gossip in my own private life so help me refrain from sowing it—for I know I will always reap what I sow (Galatians 6:7).

Strengthen me to take authority over my unruly tongue. I decree that the words of my mouth and the meditation of my heart shall be acceptable in Your sight, O Lord, my strength and my Redeemer (Psalm 19:14). In the name of Jesus, I pray. Amen.

I Need to Set Boundaries

✠ Lord, I find it hard to set limits in my relationships; consequently, my life is out of balance. I often feel resentful toward people who violate my boundaries—even though I do not do a good job expressing or clarifying them.

I realize that I act like the people of the world who say yes when they really mean no (2 Corinthians 1:17). I desire to model the behavior of Jesus who never wavered between yes and no (2 Corinthians 1:19). Help me see that even You, Father, have boundaries and consequences regarding the behavior You will tolerate from Your children—even declaring that the soul that sins will die (Ezekiel 18:20).

I ask that You give me the courage to speak up and confront people promptly, privately, and personally—the way You commanded—when they trespass against me (Matthew 18:15). Help me be clear on what I stand for and what I will and will not tolerate. Teach me to articulate my desires and preferences without fear of rejection and alienation.

Let me serve and give to others out of a pure heart rather than a desire to be loved and accepted (Romans 12:9). On the authority of Your Word, I command the spirit of fear, which has kept me from setting boundaries, to leave now. I put my trust in You; therefore, I do not fear what man can do to me (Psalm 56:11). In the name of Jesus, I pray. Amen.

I'm Brokenhearted

✚ Lord, I am heartbroken and extremely sad over the loss of my relationship with _____ . Your Word says that You are close to the brokenhearted and You rescue those who are crushed in spirit (Psalm 34:18 NLT). I need You to ease my emotional pain now. I stand on Your promise to turn my mourning into joy, comfort me, and exchange my sorrow for rejoicing (Jeremiah 31:13).

You have allowed this situation to be so, and I accept Your sovereign plan for my life. You, O Lord, are my strength and my shield; my heart trusts in You. Therefore, my heart greatly rejoices, and with my song I will praise You (Psalm 28:7). Help me not have a sad countenance, but be joyful that Your purpose is being fulfilled. Your Word says that a happy heart makes the face cheerful, but heartache crushes the spirit (Proverbs 15:13 NIV). I can't do Your will with a crushed spirit; so by Your grace I release anger, resentment, and every negative emotion associated with this heartbreak.

I thank You in advance for giving me beauty for my ashes, the oil of joy for mourning, and the garment of praise for a spirit of heaviness (Isaiah 61:3). In the name of Jesus, I pray. Amen.

*Someone I Love Has Died**

✚ O Lord, how I need You in this time of sorrow! Your Word declares that every person has an *appointed* time to die (Hebrews 9:27). I know that You are in complete control and nothing happens that You do not allow. Therefore, I ask that You help me to accept your decision to allow _____ to pass away at this time.

Lord, thank You for being my stronghold in this day of trouble (Nahum 1:7). Let Your unfailing love comfort me now just as You promised (Psalm 119:76). Help me be a source of encouragement and consolation to others who are also grieving this loss. Don't let Satan torment any of us with remorseful thoughts of what we did or did not do for _____ during his/her lifetime. I stand in faith that he/she was in right standing with You and that we will be reunited for all eternity when Jesus returns at His second coming (1 Thessalonians 4:13-18).

Now, Lord, teach those of us who remain to consider our own mortality and the brevity of life so we may apply our hearts to wisdom in how we spend our days here on earth (Psalm 90:12). In the name of Jesus, I pray. Amen.

*Can be modified to pray for relatives and friends who are grieving.

I Need to Evaluate My Expectations

✚ Lord, I have unmet expectations of certain family members, friends, work or business associates, or others in my circle of interaction. When they fail to meet my standards, I often react with impatience, anger, the silent treatment, or other ways that do not bring honor to Your name. I'm coming to You because I need wisdom on which expectations to abandon and which ones to hold fast. You promise to give me an abundance of wisdom when I ask for it (James 1:5). I lay every expectation before You now. Show me the balance.

Please do not let my fear of rejection or a negative response keep me from expressing appropriate expectations. I know that it is okay to expect my spouse to love and respect me, expect my children to submit to my authority, expect my employer to provide a safe work environment and pay a fair wage, and expect my friends to be loyal and supportive. However, I am not so clear on the matter when it boils down to my personal preferences; wanting others to comply with my traditional thinking and do things my way. Help me reach the point where I can say, "My soul, wait thou only upon God; for my expectation is from Him" (Psalm 62:5 KJV). I want to expect more from You and less from people for You are the God of all flesh and nothing or no one is too hard for You to change (Jeremiah 32:27). In the name of Jesus, I pray. Amen.

I Cannot Forgive a Hurt

✚ Father, _____ has deeply hurt me. You require me to forgive him/her or You will not forgive my sins (Matthew 6:15). You saw this transgression long before it happened, and in Your infinite wisdom, You allowed it to occur anyway. Therefore, I know that You will cause it to work for my good because I love You, and I am called according to Your purpose (Romans 8:28).

As an act of my will, I release _____ from this offense and free him/her of all obligation—even that of an apology. Your Word says that even if _____ sins against me as often as seventy times seven (490) times a day, I must forgive him/her (Matthew 18:21-22). Now, Father, You know that I could not possibly do this in my own strength; I need Your divine empowerment.

I ask You to heal my emotional pain from this hurt and keep it from scarring my heart. I give up my desire to avenge this wrong because You said that vengeance belongs to You and You will repay those who deserve it (Romans 12:19). Help me understand that forgiveness is mandatory, but reconciliation with the offender is not under certain circumstances.

I thank You for the lesson I will learn from this situation and the growth I will experience as I grant forgiveness now. In the name of Jesus, I pray. Amen.

I Need a Support System

✚ Father, I confess that I have not developed the strong support system I so desperately need. Your Word says that if I am to have friends, I must show myself friendly (Proverbs 18:24). I repent for being too busy, too distant, or too untrusting to build supportive relationships. I need You to surround me with trustworthy people who will not only help me carry my burdens, but will also keep me spiritually accountable. Give them the courage to tell me the truth about myself and let me be receptive to hearing it because You said that faithful are the wounds of a friend (Proverbs 27:6).

I reject the notion that I do not really need people in my life. Your Word warns that two are better than one because a person standing alone can be attacked and defeated, but two can stand back-to-back and conquer (Ecclesiastes 4:9,12). Please send me a few good friends who will love me at all times, those special brothers and sisters born for my adversity (Proverbs 17:17). Help me remember that Your children are to bear *one another's* burdens (Galatians 6:2). Therefore, let me put away selfishness and learn to provide mutual support. In the name of Jesus, I pray. Amen.

I Need Deliverance from Bigotry

✚ Father, I confess that I have been intolerant of those who differ from me with respect to my religion, race, or politics. I understand from Your Word that You love all men the same and there is no respect of persons with You (Romans 2:11).

Although I desire to forsake my prejudices, my thinking is entrenched. I need You to transform me by the renewing of my mind so I might prove Your good, acceptable, and perfect will (Romans 12:2).

Thank You, Father, for giving me the desire to change because it is You who works in me, both to will and to do of Your good pleasure (Philippians 2:13). Give me the courage to stop socializing with people who encourage and perpetuate prejudicial attitudes, for Your Word declares that bad company ruins good morals (1 Corinthians 15:33).

Please forgive me for all the hurt, harm, or distress I have caused others because of my biases. By Your grace I decree that I have the mind of Christ toward all Your creation (Philippians 2:5). In the name of Jesus, I pray. Amen.

Part 6

Prayers for Financial, Business, and Legal Crises

The More I Get, the More I Want

✚ Lord, You have been a faithful Father and have provided for all my needs. The problem is my eyes are never satisfied (Proverbs 27:20). I find the thrill of a new purchase very fleeting; contentment eludes me. Your Word warns that whoever loves money never has money enough, and whoever loves wealth is never satisfied with his income (Ecclesiastes 5:10). Lord, I do not want to live my life in such a meaningless way. I want to beware of and resist greed for my life does not consist in the abundance of the things I possess (Luke 12:15).

I long to be a model of godliness with contentment—this is a winning combination. Help me be content in whatever circumstances I find myself and joyful whether I have little or much (Philippians 4:11).

I realize that it is not Your will for me to be a reservoir of Your abundance, but a channel through which You can bless others. Help me understand that wealth without a purpose is just plain old materialism. Remind me often that You give me much so I can give away much (2 Corinthians 9:11). By Your grace I will focus on enriching others rather than wanting more, more, more. In the name of Jesus, I pray. Amen.

I'm Tempted to Spend Unwisely

✠ Father, I come boldly to Your throne to ask for help in this time of temptation to spend unwisely (Hebrews 4:16). Your Word reminds me that the temptations that come into my life are no different from what others experience. But You are a faithful God. You will keep the temptation from becoming so strong that I can't stand up against it. You promise to show me a way of escape so I will not give in to it (1 Corinthians 10:13).

Help me desire only those things You desire for me. I want You to be glorified in my finances. I desire to be a good steward of the resources You entrust to me. I understand that if I am untrustworthy with worldly wealth, then You will not trust me with the true riches of heaven (Luke 16:11).

I know that abundance and financial freedom will be mine as I discipline myself to abandon this and all other unwise purchases. Empower me to obey You now by walking away from this transaction. I thank You for the victory. In the name of Jesus, I pray. Amen.

I Can't Make Ends Meet

Father, I rejoice in the truth that You supply all my needs according to Your riches in glory (Philippians 4:19)—without regard to my paycheck or other expected sources of income. I need this truth to manifest now. I cannot make ends meet; however, my eyes are on You, Father. Those who seek You shall not lack any good thing (Psalm 34:10). I resist anxiety about my current shortfall in resources. Your Word says that I am to be anxious for nothing, but in everything, by prayer and supplication, with thanksgiving let my requests be made known to You and Your peace, which surpasses all understanding, will guard my heart and my mind (Philippians 4:6-7). I am requesting more funds, reduced expenses, or whatever will close the gap in my finances.

I ask for Your mercy and forgiveness for any disobedience, dishonesty, delaying, or anything else I have done wrong that has caused me to be in this situation. Teach me to always put Your financial priorities ahead of my desires and wants for Your Word declares that if I am willing and obedient, I will eat the good of the land (Isaiah 1:19).

Surround me with the favor You promised to those who are in right standing with You (Psalm 5:12). I believe Your Word that says You are able to do exceedingly abundantly above all I ask or think (Ephesians 3:20). In the name of Jesus, I pray. Amen.

Deliver Me from Debt

✚ Lord, Your Word cautions that the rich rule the poor and the borrower is servant to the lender (Proverbs 22:7). Forgive me for not heeding Your warning. I am now a financial bondservant to several creditors. I accept full responsibility for getting into this mess. I confess that I failed to delay gratification of my desires, overspent, and disobeyed Your principles of good stewardship. I repent of all past irresponsible financial behavior.

Lord, I now need You to give me the courage to face my debts and take an honest look at where I stand financially. Don't let me be in denial about the level of indebtedness I have accumulated. Let integrity guide my actions (Proverbs 11:3) as I commit to pay everyone whom I owe, including family and friends.

Lord, I do not want to be ignorant of Satan's devices (2 Corinthians 2:11). He is attempting to keep me in financial bondage—I'm paying exorbitant interest and unable to help finance Your work.

Please send a qualified person across my path to help me develop and stick to a debt-elimination strategy. Help me stop making additional credit charges. Deliver me from emotional spending. Only You can make me whole. In the name of Jesus, I pray. Amen.

Student Loans Are Ruining My Future

Father, I want to thank You for providing for my formal education through student loans. I realize that I incurred good debt in getting these loans because my education is a permanent asset and will enhance my lifetime ability to create more wealth.

Nevertheless, I am overwhelmed with the thought of repaying such a significant amount. Your Word declares that the wicked borrow and do not repay (Psalm 37:21). I do not want to dishonor Your name or my future credit worthiness by defaulting on this debt.

Help me be diligent in researching all of the options I have available, including loan consolidation, refinancing, or even taking a government-approved social service, medical, or teaching job that will reduce or eliminate the loans. Help me find the right financial advisors to give me wise input because plans go wrong for lack of advice, but many counselors bring success (Proverbs 15:22).

When I have exhausted all possibilities, help me accept the fact that the only way to eliminate the loans is to make my payments. Let me establish a workable repayment plan to eliminate this debt. Help me make the necessary lifestyle adjustments and submit extra payments when You bless me with unexpected bonuses or other income. Please bless me with a well-paying job that will keep the loan payments from becoming a hardship. In the name of Jesus, I pray. Amen.

I Do Not Have Insurance

✚ Lord, securing an insurance policy is too costly for my budget. Therefore, I am operating in faith and believing that no evil will befall me, nor will any plague come near my dwelling because You give Your angels charge over me to keep me in all my ways (Psalm 91:10-11). Besides, insurance will not protect me from accidents or calamities for You send rain on the just and on the unjust (Matthew 5:45).

Nevertheless, I do not want to be presumptuous or foolish by not having coverage, so I'm coming to You for direction. Help me be a wise steward for Your Word says that a sensible man watches for problems ahead and prepares to meet them, but the simpleton never looks and suffers the consequences (Proverbs 27:12). I know that the cost of an uninsured loss would be financially devastating.

Please lead me to an honest, caring, and astute insurance agent or financial professional who will help me determine the minimal amount of coverage I should purchase for life, disability, auto, homeowners, medical, or various other types of insurance. Show me how I can prioritize my spending, lower my deductibles, or enroll in a special plan so I can afford the related premiums. Thank You for showing Yourself strong in this situation and providing the funds I need. In the name of Jesus, I pray. Amen.

I've Misplaced Something Important

Lord, I come boldly to Your throne of grace asking for Your mercy and grace to help me find an object I have lost or misplaced (Hebrews 4:16). I repent for any carelessness or disorganization on my part that caused this to happen. Let me learn more about You as I wait for You to intervene and show Yourself strong in this situation.

How comforting it is to realize that You are all-knowing and nothing is ever hidden from You. Your Word says that You reveal deep and secret things; You know what is in the darkness, and the light dwells with You (Daniel 2:22).

I release all anxiety and frustration. I accept Your divine delay or even cancellation of my plans for I believe that You are working out a purpose that is higher and greater than my finding this item at this moment.

You said that the Holy Spirit will bring things to my remembrance (John 14:26). Help me, Holy Spirit, remember where I last had the misplaced item. I stand on Your Word believing there is nothing covered that will not be revealed and hidden that will not be known (Matthew 10:26).

Thank You in advance for being a good Father who cares about everything that pertains to me. In the name of Jesus, I pray. Amen.

My Business Is on the Decline

✝ Father, You are my refuge and strength, a present help in trouble (Psalm 46:1). Everything I have belongs to You; I am simply the steward over this business. Show Yourself strong, Lord, and turn this entity around. Just as You told Your disciples in the fishing business to launch out into the deep to experience a great catch after they had toiled all night to no avail, give me a word of instruction that will yield net-breaking results (Luke 5:4-7). Nothing is too hard for You (Jeremiah 32:27); You are the God of every circumstance and situation.

Help me trust in You with all my heart and lean not on my own understanding. In all my ways, I want to acknowledge You and allow You to direct my path. Do not let me be wise in my own eyes (Proverbs 3:5-8). Let me surround myself with wise counselors because plans fail for lack of counsel, but with many advisers they succeed (Proverbs 15:22). Reveal what adjustments I need to make in the company's products, policies, or personnel in order to be successful. Give me the courage to implement those adjustments without fear.

Most of all, Father, let Your Word always be the foundation upon which I operate this business. I commit to fairness, integrity, quality products, and good service as the trademarks of this enterprise. Let Your name be glorified as the profits help to build Your kingdom and improve the quality of life for others. In the name of Jesus, I pray. Amen.

Someone Owes Me Money

✚ Father, You saw my desire to help _____ when I advanced funds (or extended credit) to him/ her. I do not know what's happening; however, I ask that You let me do unto him/her as I would want someone to do unto me if I were in his/her position (Matthew 7:12). Help me be merciful and understanding of the circumstances outside his/her control that may be causing him/her to default on our agreement.

Although I am standing in faith to be repaid, I ask that You prepare my heart to forgive this debt in the same manner You forgive my debts of sin and rebellion against You (Matthew 6:12). I cast my care and anxiety about this situation upon You, Father, because You care for me (1 Peter 5:7) and will provide for me whether _____ pays me or not.

Now, Father, if _____ does indeed have available funds and has decided not to honor his/her obligation to me, then I ask that You help him/her realize that it is wicked to borrow and not repay (Psalm 37:21). Bring him/her to repentance so You will be honored and his/her future blessings will not be hindered. Help me not allow this situation to cause me to refrain from helping others in the future. Rather, give me a forgiving heart and a discerning spirit to know when to say yes and when to say no. In the name of Jesus, I pray. Amen.

I Need to Get Out of a Binding Contract

✚ Father, from the beginning of time, You have required that when a person swears on oath to bind himself by some agreement, he must not break his word, but must do according to all that he said (Numbers 30:2). Clearly, I am supposed to honor my oaths, vows, and agreements because my word—as well as my signature—is my bond. Notwithstanding, circumstances have changed since the signing date of a certain agreement, or I have become aware of information that shows the contract is disadvantageous to me. I need to be released from it. Yes, the other party has every right to enforce the agreement; therefore, I need their mercy and favor.

Father, I have done my best to be in right standing with You; therefore, I claim Your promise that You will bless me and surround me with favor like a shield (Psalm 5:12). I ask that You go before me, prepare the hearts of the other party to the contract, and make him/her receptive to my request for cancellation. Forgive me for not being more thorough in reviewing the terms in the first place and for not getting wise counsel to help me understand all of the contract ramifications. I do not want this situation to dishonor Your name. Therefore, cause the other party to understand and accept my justification for wanting out. Thank You for Your supernatural intervention in this situation. In the name of Jesus, I pray. Amen.

I Need Capital for My Business

✝ Lord, I'm so grateful that You have given me the courage to step outside my comfort zone and pursue this business. I acknowledge that every witty idea or invention has come from You (Proverbs 8:12 KJV).

Now, Lord, I desperately need financial capital to take the business to another level. The banks and other traditional funding sources have not been available; however, my eyes are on You alone—Jehovah-jireh, my provider (Genesis 22:14 KJV). You are able to provide exceedingly and abundantly above all I can ask or even think (Ephesians 3:20). Therefore, I ask that You send generous and godly investors who understand that the purpose of wealth is to establish Your covenant on the earth (Deuteronomy 8:18) and will embrace the vision You have given me for this enterprise. Help me be a wise and trustworthy steward of their finances.

Let me surround myself with and listen to the advice of seasoned business people because Your Word says that plans fail for lack of counsel, but with many advisers they succeed (Proverbs 15:22 NIV).

Father, I pray that You will be glorified in all of my company's policies and practices, and Your purpose will prevail in every decision. In the name of Jesus, I pray. Amen.

We Are Homeless

✚ Lord, we need a place to call our own. Your Word declares that if we seek Your kingdom, all the things we need will be added unto us (Luke 12:31). Even as You touched the innkeeper's heart to give lodging to Joseph and Mary in their time of need when all other doors were closed (Luke 2:1-7), I pray that You will move upon somebody's heart to open their doors to us or give us the funds to secure a safe place to stay.

Lord, we believe that our situation is only temporary, and in due season You will bless us exceedingly abundantly above all that we can ask or think (Ephesians 3:20) for it is Your pleasure to give good things to Your children (Matthew 7:11). We pray a special blessing in advance for those who will extend kindness to us during this time. Your Word declares that he who helps the needy lends to You, and You will repay (Proverbs 19:17). We ask that You multiply their generosity back to them a hundredfold.

Forgive us for any poor decisions we made that resulted in our being in this situation. Grant us mercy and teach us how to be good stewards of Your money—and our relationships with others because a brother is born for such an adversity as we are experiencing (Proverbs 17:17). In the name of Jesus, I pray. Amen.

I'm Thinking About Filing for Bankruptcy

✝ Lord, I am in a predicament because I cannot meet my financial obligations as they become due. I realize that when I incurred these debts, I made an implied vow to repay them and, therefore, must now make every effort to keep my promise and pay what I owe. Your Word declares that living on credit and not paying my debts is characteristic of the wicked for they borrow and do not repay (Psalm 37:21).

I do not want to use bankruptcy as a quick fix to avoid the responsibility of working through my debts. Please grant me a miracle just as You did for the widow whom You enabled to pay her deceased husband's debts, thereby saving her sons from imprisonment by the creditors (2 Kings 4:1-7). I know that my Christian witness is on the line because most people view bankruptcy as evidence of financial irresponsibility. Help me make the radical and necessary lifestyle adjustments and commit to Your financial priorities. Let me proceed in filing the bankruptcy petition only if this situation is truly due to circumstances beyond my control. Otherwise, I ask that You surround me with favor (Psalm 5:12) as I contact all of my creditors and negotiate a payout for my outstanding balances. In the name of Jesus, I pray. Amen.

I'm Going to Court

✝ Father, the legal issue I am facing must now be decided in a court of law. My faith is not in the skill of my attorney, the ethnic or gender makeup of the jury, or the reputation of the judge because they are all vessels in Your hand. I confidently decree a favorable decision on my behalf for, as one in right standing with You, I am surrounded with Your favor like a shield (Psalm 5:12). I ask that You reveal every deep and secret thing relating to this matter; You know what is in the darkness for the light dwells with You (Daniel 2:22).

Your Word says that You hate a false witness who pours out lies (Proverbs 6:16,19). I bind every lying spirit that will present itself in this case. I decree that every witness for the defense *and* the prosecution will tell the truth. According to Your Word, no weapon formed against me will prevail, and I will refute every tongue that accuses me. This is a benefit I enjoy as Your servant—You will vindicate me (Isaiah 54:17). You execute righteousness and justice for all who are oppressed (Psalm 103:6). I honor You, Father, as the ultimate unbiased Judge. There is no partiality or respect of persons with You; whoever does wrong shall be repaid for the wrong he has done (Colossians 3:25). Therefore, I will rest in the assurance of Your Word and expect a positive outcome. In the name of Jesus, I pray. Amen.

Part 7

Prayers for School, Job, and Work Crises

I Need Grace to Pass an Exam

O God, what peace and comfort there is to know that You are all-knowing and there is never a question that can baffle You. Therefore, I come boldly to Your throne of grace so that I may obtain mercy and find grace to help me pass this very important exam (Hebrews 4:16). Yes, I'm doing my part by studying, but I am not trusting in myself for a successful outcome because Your Word says that he who trusts in himself is a fool (Proverbs 28:26).

My eyes are on the Holy Spirit to show me what I do not know and bring everything I study to my remembrance (John 14:26). I praise You, Father, for You give wisdom to the wise and knowledge to those who have understanding. You reveal deep and secret things; You know what is in the darkness, and light dwells with You (Daniel 2:21-22). I stand in faith that You will reveal the answers to whatever part of the exam that I find myself in darkness.

I thank You and praise You in advance, O God, for giving me wisdom, insight, and making known to me the answers to the exam (Daniel 2:23). I will give You all the glory and will resist any pride as a result of this victory. In the name of Jesus, I pray. Amen.

I Feel Unsafe at School

✚ Father, along with the other students, I have come to this place of learning to get an education. As such, we need to be able to attend classes without the fear of someone perpetrating violence against us. I know that Satan walks about like a roaring lion, seeking whom he may devour (1 Peter 5:8-9). He comes to steal, kill, and destroy (John 10:10). However, on the authority of Your Word, I bind the spirit of violence from this campus. I decree that Satan will not steal lives, kill dreams, or destroy the reputation of this school with violence.

I ask You to touch and heal the distorted minds of those who would want to harm us. Foil their plans, Father. Expose every person who is a threat to this campus. Let the administration and legal authorities deal with each one swiftly and wisely so no lives will be lost. Send someone across the path of every potential perpetrator to convince them to get professional and spiritual help.

Rather than causing anxiety, I pray that the potential threat of violence will cause students, faculty, administration officials, and parents to draw close to You and learn how to stand in faith for Your protection. What Satan means for bad, turn it into good and let a spiritual revival break out on this campus. In the name of Jesus, I pray. Amen.

I Have to Make a Speech

✚ Father, I acknowledge You as the supplier of all my needs (Philippians 4:19). Right now I need courage and confidence. I have to make a speech or presentation, and anxiety about my ability to perform well is trying to invade my mind. Forgive me for entertaining thoughts of inadequacy when Your Word clearly states that my competence or sufficiency does not originate in me, but it is from You only (2 Corinthians 3:5-6).

Father, although the Holy Spirit is my helper, I understand that I must do my part by diligently preparing for this engagement. I want my presentation to inform, inspire, and impact the audience in a lasting way.

Thank You for this door of opportunity that You have opened for me to influence others with my words. Lord, give me Your words to speak for they accomplish what You please and yield positive results (Isaiah 55:11).

Thank You for the peace that comes with relying on Your promises. In the name of Jesus, I pray. Amen.

I Feel Inadequate for This Assignment

✚ Lord, I have been charged with a task that I feel totally inadequate to perform. I realize this is a great opportunity for me to allow You to show Yourself strong in my life because Your strength is made perfect in my weakness (2 Corinthians 12:9). I understand from Your Word that I am not adequate in myself to consider anything as originating from myself, but my adequacy is from You (2 Corinthians 3:5). Therefore, I take my eyes off my limitations and focus on You—my all-knowing, all-powerful, and always-present Father. I let go of all anxiety about this task because when You begin a good work in me, You are faithful to complete it (Philippians 1:6). I cannot fail.

Lord, teach me how to encourage myself from the numerous accounts of Your great feats recorded in the Bible. Help me comprehend the truth that You are the same yesterday, today, and forever (Hebrews 13:8). Therefore, just as You empowered David to slay Goliath, You can help me conquer every giant or seemingly insurmountable task. In fact, I am more than a conqueror through You (Romans 8:37).

Let me always choose to stay connected to You. Your Word declares that You are the vine, I am the branch, and if I remain in You, I will produce much fruit for apart from You I can do nothing (John 15:5). In the name of Jesus, I pray. Amen.

I Lost My Job

Lord, I am really hurt and disappointed because management terminated me from my job. I know it did not come as a surprise to You for You know everything. In fact Your Word says that all the days ordained for me were written in Your book before one of them came to pass (Psalm 139:16). I can only conclude then, that You have better plans for me; plans to help me and not to harm me, plans to give me a future and a hope (Jeremiah 29:11).

Please forgive me for looking at my job as if it were my source, when in fact it was just a chosen channel of Your provision for a chosen season. Oh, for grace to trust You more! I know that You can give me favor with men and can open doors no man can close. Therefore, I will not worry or dwell on Satan-inspired scenarios of lack and potential homelessness. I will declare that all my needs are met according to Your riches in heaven (Philippians 4:19)—versus my paycheck.

Help me be sensitive to Your voice as You direct me to my next assignment. Whether it is employment with a company or ownership of my own business, one thing I am certain—You will never leave nor forsake me (Hebrews 13:5). In the name of Jesus, I pray. Amen.

My Boss Is a Nightmare

Lord, I am grateful to have a job. I desire to obey Your command to submit to those who have authority over me because the authorities that exist have been established by You. I understand that if I rebel against authority, I am rebelling against what You have instituted and will bring judgment on myself (Romans 13:1-2). My boss makes obeying this command very difficult. Therefore, I'm bringing this situation to You because nothing is too hard for You (Jeremiah 32:27). I pray that You will touch his/her heart and save his/her soul. Teach him/her how to manage people and processes with care, tact, and wisdom.

Search my heart and help me see if my behavior contributes in any way to his/her harsh or unfair treatment (Psalm 139:23-24). Help me not project a bad or insubordinate attitude. Cause me to be a team player, do my work with all diligence, and comply with all policies and procedures.

Give me favor with my boss and teach me how to accept his/her decisions without becoming cynical or complaining to others. Let my light shine before him/her so he/she may see my good works and glorify You (Matthew 5:16). In the name of Jesus, I pray. Amen.

My Performance Is Poor at Work

Father, I confess I have not carried out my assigned duties with diligence and excellence. Forgive me, Lord, for this dishonoring testimony. Reveal to me the root cause of my behavior—whether it is just pure laziness, subtle retaliation for management's unfairness, job dissatisfaction, or other causes. I know that none of these reasons justifies my actions because Your Word says that I should work heartily as unto You and not to men, knowing You will reward me (Colossians 3:22-23).

From this day forward, I want to be a model employee. Help me be satisfied with this job until You direct me elsewhere. Teach me how to effectively communicate my concerns and wishes. Work in me the desire to please my superiors—even when they are not looking (Ephesians 6:5)—to do whatever is asked, comply with company policies, and do it all with a good attitude. Let my presence bring blessings to the company just as You blessed Potiphar's house simply because he put Joseph in charge of his affairs (Genesis 39:5). I realize that, as a confessed believer, every action on my part either exalts or diminishes Your name to the observing world. I want my performance to show that I have Your spirit of excellence. In the name of Jesus, I pray. Amen.

I'm Overloaded with Work

✚ Lord, I have more work to do than I can handle. You said that when I am heavy ladened with work, I should come to You and You will give me rest for my soul (Matthew 11:28). You know what portion of this load is within my control, and what portion is not. Give me the wisdom to evaluate all my responsibilities and be honest with myself about why I am in this predicament. Your Word says that I should not wear myself out to get rich, but have the wisdom to show restraint (Proverbs 23:4). Show me where I may be sacrificing my peace, health, or relationships on the altar of "more money." If my load is due to my failure to delegate properly, deliver me from this destructive behavior. Help me heed the advice Jethro gave to Moses in the wilderness—to delegate lesser matters to qualified others and handle only the weightier issues myself (Exodus 18:17-22).

Finally, if I am overworked because I have refused to ask for help, or I simply derive esteem from being Superman/Superwoman, then heal me from my flawed thinking. Help me keep life in perspective on a daily basis, realize that there is nothing better than to enjoy the fruit of my labor, and find satisfaction in work because this pleasure is from Your hand (Ecclesiastes 2:24). In the name of Jesus, I pray. Amen.

I Can't Stay Focused

✚ Father, my thoughts are scattered in every direction, and I can't seem to stay focused on any course of action. I know that this is evidence that I am leaning to my own understanding and failing to acknowledge You in all my ways because when I do, You promise to direct my path (Proverbs 3:5-6). Please forgive me if I am trying to forge an agenda that has not originated with You. Teach me how to be still and hear Your voice when You say, "This is the way, walk in it" (Isaiah 30:21).

Help me take my wandering thoughts captive and make them obedient to Christ (2 Corinthians 10:5). I place every plan in my heart before You now. I know that in the final analysis, it is only Your purpose that will prevail (Proverbs 19:21).

By the power of Your Holy Spirit, I will look straight ahead and fix my eyes on what lies before me. I will follow Your lead and mark out a straight path for my feet; then stick to the path. I refuse to be sidetracked any longer (Proverbs 4:25-27). In the name of Jesus, I pray. Amen.

My Subordinate Is Disrespectful

Father, I thank You for trusting me with this management position. I want to honor You by being a strong and competent leader. My concern today is that my subordinate has become disrespectful of my authority. I know that if I allow him/her to continue in this vein, the other employees may attempt to emulate his/her conduct or lose respect for me. I am hurt, angered, and offended by his/her actions. According to Your Word, I must confront him privately and personally (Matthew 18:15). I need Your wisdom and courage to do that. But before I do that, Father, I ask You to search my heart and reveal where I may have failed, disappointed, or offended him/her in some way. Your Word commands me to treat employees right and refrain from threatening them because we have the same Master in heaven who has no favorites (Ephesians 6:9).

Father, you know the personal and professional issues, failures, or disappointments that are plaguing _____. Draw him/her to Yourself and heal his/her pain. Help me show my concern without compromising the company's standards for excellence and proper protocol between bosses and subordinates. Give me the courage to make whatever decision is necessary to resolve this problem by doing what is right versus what is safe or convenient. In the name of Jesus, I pray. Amen.

Dirty Politics Are Threatening My Career

Father, You see the coworkers who are rising against me because I'm on the fast track. What they do not understand is that my career is in Your hands. I know that You have plans for me; plans to prosper me and not to harm me, plans to give me a hope and a future (Jeremiah 29:11). Therefore, who can thwart what You have purposed? When You stretch Your hand out, who can turn it back (Isaiah 14:27)?

I pray that You give me the grace to respond to my detractors in a way that will bring honor to Your name—and enhance my witness for You. Let anger and bitterness be far from me. Help me remember that no weapon formed against me will prevail. I will refute every tongue that rises against me—this is one of my benefits as Your child—and You will vindicate me on every side (Isaiah 54:17).

Help me be like Daniel and maintain a consistent devotional life, do my work with excellence, and keep a good attitude—in the midst of dirty politics designed to thwart my promotions (Daniel 6:1-24). Thank You, Father, that promotion comes neither from the east, nor from the west, nor from the south. You are the Judge; You put down one and exalt another (Psalm 75:6-7). In the name of Jesus, I pray. Amen.

Someone in Authority Wants Me to Compromise My Values

Lord, Your Word says that the integrity of the upright will guide them (Proverbs 11:3). You know that I have purposed in my heart to walk in integrity in all my endeavors. Now _____ has made a request that will require me to compromise my moral convictions and violate Your Word. Give me the wisdom and the resolve of Daniel who purposed in his heart not to eat the king's defiled meat when he was required to do so (Daniel 1:8). Your Word promises that with every temptation You make a way of escape so I need not succumb to it (1 Corinthians 10:13). Show me a way out that will solve the problem at hand without my sinning against You.

Father, do not let me lean on my own understanding by rationalizing options that are not totally in line with Your Word because partial obedience is disobedience. Even if my decision results in my being penalized, terminated, or alienated, please give me the courage to do the right thing and make the choice that honors You. My eyes are on You. You know how to deliver the godly out of temptation (2 Peter 2:9). Let the resolution of this matter be a testimony of Your favor and faithfulness to those who trust in You. In the name of Jesus, I pray. Amen.

I'm a Victim of Discrimination

Lord, Your Word says that to show partiality or have respect of persons is not good (Proverbs 28:21). You see that _____ is attempting to disadvantage me because of my race, sex, or age. Clearly such behavior is displeasing to You because You do not show favoritism but accept everybody who fears You and does what is right (Acts 10:34-35). Therefore, I pray that You will bring conviction to the hearts of all parties involved in this discrimination. Let the fear of You come upon them; let them judge me objectively because with You there is no injustice or partiality (2 Chronicles 19:7).

Help _____ see that we are all Your children, the sheep of Your pasture, and You have made me whatever way I am (Psalm 100:3)—even if I am different from his/her preference. Cause him/her to understand that in Your kingdom, it does not matter if you are a Jew or a Gentile, circumcised or uncircumcised, barbaric or civilized, slave or free, or different in any other way. Christ is all that matters, and He lives in all of us (Colossians 3:11).

Give me the grace to forgive and to extend Your love to everyone involved in the situation. I stand on Your Word that proclaims no one can disadvantage me or thwart Your purpose for my life (Isaiah 14:27). In the name of Jesus, I pray. Amen.

I Want a Promotion

✚ Father, Your Word declares that I am not to be anxious for anything, but in everything by prayer and supplication, with thanksgiving, let my request be made known unto You (Philippians 4:6). My request is for a job promotion. I am encouraged by the truth that promotion comes neither from the east, nor from the west, nor from the south. But You are the Judge; You can put down one person and set up another in their place—according to Your will (Psalm 75:6-7).

You said that we have not because we ask not (James 4:2). When I make my request, give me the courage and the right words to say to my boss. Let me objectively and accurately discuss my contribution to the company, my achievements, and the value of my knowledge and performance rather than my financial need. Cleanse me of any impure motives for wanting this promotion—You said that I ask amiss if I plan to spend what I get on my pleasures (James 4:3).

Help me always model the example of Daniel by working with a spirit of excellence, being faithful, honest, responsible, and giving no occasion to my enemies who look to find fault with my performance (Daniel 6:4-6). Most of all help me resist pride in being promoted. Please do not let me become overwhelmed with my new responsibilities to the point that I become slack in praying and reading Your Word. In the name of Jesus, I pray. Amen.

Part 8

Prayers for Emotional Crises

Shyness Is Ruining My Life

✚ Father, I am tired of sitting on the social sidelines of life watching other people get to know each other and develop mutually beneficial relationships. I find myself wanting to engage others in conversation, but I can't think of anything to say. There have been times when I knew I had meaningful and helpful information to share, but I kept quiet. I am plagued with the fear of making a fool of myself, appearing unintelligent, or receiving a negative response from others. Lord, Your Word declares that You are my light and my salvation. Whom shall I fear? You are the strength of my life; of whom shall I be afraid? (Psalm 27:1). I want to start now to cast down negative imaginations and everything that rises up against what I know about You and bring every thought into obedience of Christ (2 Corinthians 10:5).

Lord, I know that You have not given me a spirit of timidity, but a spirit of power, of love, and of self-discipline (2 Timothy 1:7). I realize that if I allow shyness to hold me prisoner to things I want to do and say, I will never be the effective and assertive leader You have already equipped me to be. Therefore, I claim the promise You made to a fearful Moses—to be with his mouth and to teach him what to say (Exodus 4:12). In the name of Jesus, I pray. Amen.

I'm Having Thoughts of Suicide

✚ Lord, I'm coming to You in my hopelessness and despair. Satan has put thoughts into my mind; thoughts of ending it all by taking my own life. Although Your Word warns that I am not to be ignorant of his devices (2 Corinthians 2:11), I have allowed myself to be pulled into his vacuum of depression and discouragement. I know that You gave me the gift of life for a purpose, and I do not have the right to decide when my time is up.

Your Word declares that You have plans for me; plans to prosper me and not to harm me, plans to give me hope and a future (Jeremiah 29:11). Lord, I want to believe this; please help my unbelief (Mark 9:24). Hear my cry for I am very low. Rescue me from this pit of despair. Bring my soul out of prison so I can praise You (Psalm 142:6-7).

Help me cast down every thought that comes to remind me of past negative events that keep me in emotional bondage. I am determined to overcome by the blood of Jesus and the words of my testimony (Revelation 7:14). Therefore, I decree by faith that I am free of suicidal thoughts. The Son has set me free, and I am free indeed (John 8:36). In the name of Jesus, I pray. Amen.

I'm Overwhelmed with Life's Pressures

✚ Lord, I am beset with trouble. It seems as if more problems arise each day. I am weary of my own sighing and can find no rest (Jeremiah 45:3). From the end of the earth, I will cry to You. When my heart is overwhelmed, lead me to the rock that is higher than I. You have been a shelter for me, a strong tower from the enemy (Psalm 61:2-3). It seems that the weight of the world is on my shoulders. I know that this is not Your will. Please teach me how to cast all my cares and concerns upon You for You care about what happens to me (1 Peter 5:7). Give me the courage to change the things that I can, the grace to accept the things that I cannot, and the wisdom to know the difference.

Let me bring glory to Your name by doing *only* the things You have told me to do (John 17:4) instead of being stretched in every direction by the wishes and demands of others. As pressure and stress bear down on me, let me find joy in Your commands (Psalm 119:143).

Lord, do not allow me to become so busy that I eliminate my quiet time with You. Teach me how to be still and know that You are God (Psalm 46:10). Thank You for being my refuge, a very present help in a time of trouble (Psalm 46:1). In the name of Jesus, I pray. Amen.

I'm About to Explode with Anger

✝ Lord, You gave me the emotion of anger for Your righteous purpose; therefore, I know that *becoming* angry is not wrong. However, in Your Word You warned that I should not sin by letting anger gain control over me for in so doing, I give Satan a foothold in my life (Ephesians 4:26-27).

Help me cease being angry and to turn from my rage now for it can only lead to physical and emotional harm to me and others (Psalm 37:8). Teach me how to release my anger before You in prayer. Help me remember that You are the avenger of every wrong perpetrated against me (Romans 12:19). Therefore, I do not have to render evil for evil. I do not want to respond in a way that dishonors You and destroys my Christian witness. Your Word says only a fool gives full vent to his anger, but a wise man keeps himself under control (Proverbs 29:11).

Change my heart, O God. Help me develop patience and long-suffering. Show me how to handle difficult situations with tact and wisdom. Most of all, empower me to demonstrate the kind of love that covers a multitude of sins, looks beyond faults, and sees the real needs of others (1 Peter 4:8). Thank You for the victory over destructive anger. In the name of Jesus, I pray. Amen.

The Spirit of Fear Is Attacking My Mind

Dear Lord, the spirit of fear has come to overtake me. Your Word assures me that it is not from You (2 Timothy 1:7). I know that when I seek Your face, You hear me and deliver me from all my fears (Psalm 34:4). Therefore, I cast down every anxious thought that rises up against what I know about You and Your power (2 Corinthians 10:5). I stand on Your promise that You will never leave me nor forsake me (Hebrews 13:5).

I rest in the truth that nothing is too hard for You (Jeremiah 32:27); You are in complete control of this situation. Thank You in advance for working things out for my good according to Your divine plan and purpose (Romans 8:28). I rejoice in knowing that You have already given Your angels responsibility for keeping me and protecting me in all my ways (Psalm 91:11). I resist the spirit of fear now and command it to flee (James 4:7). By faith I decree that Your peace, which surpasses my understanding, will guard my heart and my mind (Philippians 4:7). Therefore, I will not let my heart be troubled, neither will I let it be afraid (John 14:27). In the name of Jesus, I pray. Amen.

I'm Depressed

O Lord, my soul melts from heaviness; I need You to strengthen me according to Your Word (Psalm 119:28). If this depression is a result of a physical disorder, then I ask You to heal me through a miracle or the right medical prescription, vitamins, or herbs—for You are the ultimate source of my wholeness.

Lord, help me understand that, like my body, my mind requires nutritious input to be healthy. Empower me to resist the mental junk food of guilt, bitterness, hopelessness, perfectionism, and negative thoughts that lead to depression. Give me a desire to feed on Your Word and focus only on the things that are true, honest, just, pure, lovely, and of a good report (Philippians 4:8). Help me spend more time with You for in Your presence there is fullness of joy (Psalm 16:11). Yes, Lord, Your joy is my strength (Nehemiah 8:10).

This is the day You have made; I will rejoice and be glad in it (Psalm 118:24). Help me start focusing on the plans You have for me, plans to give me a hope and a future (Jeremiah 29:11). With the help of the Holy Spirit, I will continually offer a sacrifice of praise to You by proclaiming the glory of Your name (Hebrews 13:15). Thank You for anointing me now with the oil of gladness (Hebrews 1:9). In the name of Jesus, I pray. Amen.

I'm Unbearably Lonely

✚ Father, I feel isolated, excluded, and estranged from meaningful relationships. I know that You are always with me, and You will never leave nor forsake me (Hebrews 13:5). Notwithstanding, You created me to be a social, relational being in need of interaction with other people. I know that living as an island unto myself is against Your will and purpose for humankind (Genesis 2:18).

Please help me acknowledge and forsake any negative behavior on my part that may cause people not to embrace me, such as being critical, judgmental, argumentative, or unforgiving. Give me the tongue of the learned so I will speak appropriate words in season to others. Also open my ears to listen to their issues with a genuine interest (Isaiah 50:4). Give me a desire to use my unique spiritual and natural gifts to serve and enhance the quality of life for others.

Your Word says that if I want friends, I must show myself friendly (Proverbs 18: 24). Help me take the initiative to connect with positive, trustworthy people whom I can fellowship with on a regular basis. Teach me how to accept their love, generosity, and support. Help me understand the importance of nurturing my relationships and not just connecting with friends when it is convenient for me. Most of all let me experience the comfort of Your Holy Spirit. In the name of Jesus, I pray. Amen.

I Need Healing from Childhood Sexual Abuse

✚ Lord, only You know the anguish I have suffered from being sexually abused. I understand that I should not blame myself for the evil choice the offender made to violate me, neither do I want to keep focusing on the person(s) in my life who should have protected me but did not. I'm ready to allow You to break the mental, emotional, and even physical chains of the abuse. O Lord, bring my soul—my mind, my will, my emotions—out of prison so I may praise Your name (Psalm 142:7).

I take authority over the constant memories of the abuse. I decree that they are dead; they shall not live because You have made them perish and relinquish their power (Isaiah 26:14). They will no longer dictate my attitude or my actions toward the opposite sex. I forgive everybody associated with the abuse. I ask that You convict them of their wrongdoing and save their souls.

Please use my deliverance to bring freedom to others who have suffered similarly as I testify of Your power to heal the broken in heart and bind their wounds (Psalm 147:3). In the name of Jesus, I pray. Amen.

I'm Consumed with Envy

Lord, You desire me to be honest in my heart (Psalm 51:6) and confess my sins so You can cleanse me from all unrighteousness (1 John 1:9). I confess that I have allowed envy to get a stronghold in my life. I find myself withdrawing from and feeling ill will toward certain people because of their physical, financial, social, professional, intellectual, residential, or other good fortune and advantage. I acknowledge that my feelings are rooted in my discontentment or frustration with my current experience in the areas where I envy others. Of course I realize that there may be aspects of my life others desire to have. Give me the humility and the wisdom not to inspire envy by boasting or flaunting my advantage.

Your Word says that envy rots the bones (Proverbs 14:30)—eroding the very foundation of my existence. Help me put envy far from me for where envying and strife are, there are confusion and every evil work (James 3:16). Let me use the temptation to envy as motivation to make the necessary changes in my life. Most of all give me the grace and the wisdom to accept Your sovereign plan for my life and be content with such things that I have for godliness with contentment is great gain (1 Timothy 6:6). I decree that gratitude will be my daily attitude. In the name of Jesus, I pray. Amen.

Jealousy Keeps Rearing Its Head

✚ Lord, I'm concerned that I may be displaced professionally, socially, or in any special relationship. I know that my feelings are rooted in fear. I am reminded that You have not given me the spirit of fear; but of power, and of love, and of a sound mind (2 Timothy 1:7). Therefore, I resist this unwelcome intrusion from Satan and command it to go. Father, help me comprehend the truth. Whatever You have destined for me, You maintain my lot; You guard all that is mine (Psalm 16:5).

Teach me how to bring my fears to You and refrain from smothering or controlling others because I do not want to lose their affection. Let me begin to enjoy my various relationships without competing for attention or superiority in any area or fearing that someone else will be more highly esteemed.

I claim Your Word that says as I seek You, You will hear me and deliver me from all my fears (Psalm 34:4). I'm ready to stop living with the anxiety of inadequacy. Cause me to embrace the sobering truth that I am not adequate in myself to think any good thing originating from me; but my sufficiency is of God (2 Corinthians 3:5). Help me acknowledge and appreciate the treasures You have deposited inside me so I can come to any relationship with a healthy sense of self-worth. In the name of Jesus, I pray. Amen.

Guilt Is Tormenting Me

✚ O God, despite the fact that I have repented and sincerely regret my actions, the guilt of my sin continues to torment me. This burden is too heavy to bear any longer (Psalm 38:4).

Your Word declares that You are ready to forgive and have abundant mercy toward all who call upon You (Psalm 86:5). The problem is that I'm having difficulty releasing myself from the remorse of my sin. Please help me comprehend the truth that when I confess my sin, You are faithful and just to forgive me and to cleanse me from all unrighteousness (1 John 1:9). By the power of Your Spirit, I will no longer let thoughts of guilt destroy my peace. I will stand on Your declaration—as far as the east is from the west, so far have You removed my transgressions from me (Psalm 103:12).

Thank You, Father, for casting my sin into the depths of the sea (Micah 7:19) never to be remembered again (Hebrews 10:17). And since You do not remember it, help me to stop rehearsing it. I decree now that I am forgiven by the blood Jesus shed for me on Calvary. In the name of Jesus, I pray. Amen.

Deliver Me from Pornography

✚ Father, I'm in a spiritual and emotional crisis because I have opened the door for Satan to gain a stronghold in my life. I realize that I commit adultery in my heart every time I look at a woman with lust (Matthew 5:28). I ask that You have mercy on me because of Your unfailing love. Because of Your great compassion, blot out the stain of my sin. Wash me clean from my guilt. Purify me from my sin (Psalm 51:1-2).

Help me stop making provisions to fulfill the lust of my flesh by what I expose myself to through movies, television, the Internet, adult magazines, or any other medium (Romans 13:14). I repent and ask for Your deliverance now.

Show me the emotional need I'm really trying to fulfill. Give me the courage, the wisdom, and the strength to deal with it in a way that honors You. I want to follow the example of Job who made a covenant with his eyes not to look with lust upon a woman (Job 31:1). I can't do this in my own strength so please fill me with Your Spirit. Give me a desire for You that will transcend and demolish all lustful thoughts. In the name of Jesus, I pray. Amen.

I'm Battling Sexual Addiction

✚ Father, my spirit is indeed willing to obey You, but my flesh is weak when it comes to sexual addiction (Matthew 26:41). You know the biological, psychological, or spiritual reasons for this compulsion. Fill the empty places in my emotions and help me cope with life's stressors in a God-honoring way.

Your Word says that if I confess my sin, You are faithful and just to forgive me and to cleanse me from all unrighteousness (1 John 1:9). I realize that I have failed to maintain right standing with You after You have cleansed me. Forgive me, Lord, for sinning against You and against my own body (1 Corinthians 6:18). I sincerely want to get out of this cycle of repenting and relapsing.

Help me realize that I cannot conquer this addiction with sheer willpower alone. I acknowledge that I am hopeless without You and the support of others. Please direct me to a godly counselor or group who will keep me accountable and focused on You.

By faith I decree that this sin will not reign in my body and cause me to obey its lusts. I will not present my body as an instrument of unrighteousness to sin, but as an instrument of righteousness to God. Therefore, this sin shall not have dominion over me (Romans 6:12-14). In the name of Jesus, I pray. Amen.

I'm Caught in a Cycle of Masturbation

✚ Father, I've fallen into the habit of satisfying my sexual desire outside the context of marriage. I know that when I use what You created in a way that is contrary to Your purpose, I enter the realm of abuse. Forgive me for misusing my sexual organs. I realize that if I continue in this vein, masturbation can become an addiction. Further, because my focus is only on bringing *me* pleasure, it can train me to become selfish in marital sex. Therefore, I ask that You direct my steps by Your Word and let not this behavior have dominion over me (Psalm 119:133).

I know that fantasizing, pornography, books, magazines, TV shows, and numerous other stimuli give rise to my urge to masturbate. Give me the strength to slam every door I have opened that inspires my behavior. Help me stop setting vile or wicked things before my eyes (Psalm 101:3). Reveal the negative emotions I'm attempting to pacify by masturbating and teach me how to deal with them in a God-honoring way.

I realize that my most important sex organ is my mind because my thoughts control my sexual arousal. So, right now I submit my mind to the Holy Spirit to produce the fruit of self-control in me (Galatians 5:22-23). Father, let the very thought of masturbating become repulsive to me. I thank You now for transforming me by the renewing of my mind (Romans 12:2). In the name of Jesus, I pray. Amen.

I'm Trapped in Grief

✚ Lord, I realize that by now, my grief over _____'s death should have subsided to some extent. Clearly, I have not come to the place of acceptance of Your will in his/her death. Help me know that _____'s life span was already predetermined by You (Psalm 139:16) and I could do nothing to impact or change that. I do not want to grieve as those with no hope for I believe I will see him/her again (1 Thessalonians 4:13).

Help me, Lord. I cannot break these chains of sorrow alone. Your Word says that a brother is born for adversity (Proverb 17:17); therefore, I ask that You lead me to a person, counselor, or support group that can help me identify the unfulfilled need or other unfinished business that is keeping me in the clutches of grief.

By the power You have given to me as a believer, I take authority over this grieving spirit. I decree that the peace of God, which surpasses all understanding, is guarding my heart and my mind through Christ Jesus (Philippians 4:7). By Your grace I will continue to cherish _____'s memory while moving forward in fulfilling my divine purpose and destiny. In the name of Jesus, I pray. Amen.

I Need Deliverance from Nicotine, Alcohol, or Drugs

Father, it's time for me to mortify the deeds of my body so I may live (Romans 8:13). I am tired of the physical and psychological struggle of this addiction. I admit that I am powerless over it in my own strength. I realize that You are my only hope and apart from You I can do nothing (John 15:5). I make a commitment now to turn my will over to You.

Empower me not only to say no to Satan's temptation, but to say an even stronger yes to You and Your plan for my life. Please do not banish me from Your presence and do not take Your Holy Spirit from me (Psalm 51:11) for where Your Spirit is, there is freedom (2 Corinthians 3:17). Lord, You know the void I am trying to fill with this substance. Please do not let it have dominion over me (Proverbs 23:2). Take away my desire and help me resist the cravings.

Teach me how to walk in victory on a day-by-day basis rather than thinking that I can solve this problem all at once. I know that if the Son makes me free, I shall be free indeed (John 8:36). Thank You in advance for making me more than a conqueror (Romans 8:37). In the name of Jesus, I pray. Amen.

My Mental Fog Is Alarming

✝ Lord, as each day passes, it seems like I become more forgetful and experience an overall mental fog. I refuse to conform to the world's belief that mental decline is part of normal aging for I have been transformed by the renewing of my mind (Romans 12:2). I have the mind of Christ (1 Corinthians 2:16).

Help me stop multi-tasking, overloading my schedule, failing to plan, and engaging in other behaviors that keep my mind overcrowded and unfocused on the task at hand. Help me commit my works unto You so You will establish my thoughts (Proverbs 16:3). Give me the discipline to exercise, get proper rest, drink plenty of water, and make wise food choices that enhance my mental alertness. Finally, help me remember that meditating on Your Word makes me wise and increases my understanding (Psalm 119:97-100).

Thank You, Father, that I do not have to walk in the spirit of fear of a mental decline because You have given me a spirit of power, love, and a sound mind (2 Timothy 1:7). I am resting on Your promise that the Holy Spirit will teach me and bring all things to my remembrance when I need to recall them (John 14:26). In the name of Jesus, I pray. Amen.

Part 9

Prayers for Church, Country, and Other Crises

Discord Is Destroying Our Church

✚ O Lord, an evil spirit has come in to destroy the unity of our church. How good and pleasant it would be if we would just dwell together in unity for that is where You command Your blessings (Psalm 133:1,3). Help us see that our infighting is a Satanic tactic to hinder our prayers, get our focus off of lost souls, and make us ineffective examples of Christianity.

Teach us how to respect and appreciate each others' talents, perspectives, and positions rather than envy them. For where envying and strife exist, there are confusion and every evil work (James 3:16). Show us how to disagree without being disagreeable. Let us walk worthy of our calling as Your children with all lowliness and gentleness, with long-suffering, bearing with one another in love, and making every effort to keep the unity of the Spirit in the bond of peace (Ephesians 4:1-4).

By the authority which You have given to me as a believer, I bind egos, pride, vain ambition, envy, jealousy, and every evil spirit that is trying to thwart Your work. I loose the spirit of unity, love, and long-suffering (Matthew 18:18). I stand on Your Word and declare that this is Your church and the gates of hell shall not prevail against it (Matthew 16:18). In the name of Jesus, I pray. Amen.

Missionaries Are in Danger

Lord, thank You for the selfless decision these missionaries made to risk their lives and spread Your Gospel. I stand on Your promise that You will never leave nor forsake them (Hebrews 13:5). Let Your peace, which passes all understanding, keep their hearts and their minds during this crisis (Philippians 4:7).

Your Word declares that Your eyes run to and fro throughout the whole earth to show Yourself strong on behalf of those whose hearts are loyal to You (2 Chronicles 16:9). Show Yourself strong on behalf of these committed servants, Father. You are the God of all flesh and nothing is too hard for You (Jeremiah 32:27).

I take authority over every opposing force that comes to hinder their work. I remind Satan that he is a defeated foe for You have given Your servants power to tread on serpents, scorpions, and over all the power of the enemy—nothing shall by any means hurt them (Luke 10:19).

I pray that their resolve be strong and their faith unwavering. What the enemy meant for bad, Father, turn it into good. I know and declare that all things are working together for the good of these missionaries because they love You and are called according to Your purpose (Romans 8:28). In the name of Jesus, I pray. Amen.

My Church Is in Urgent Need of Finances

Lord, my church needs funds now to fulfill Your mandate. I know that You can and will supply every need according to Your riches in heaven (Philippians 4:19). You never give any person or organization a responsibility without giving them the ability to respond. When You begin a good work, You are faithful to complete it (Philippians 1:6). I ask that You touch the hearts of generous and obedient people and give them a burden to finance this work.

Help the leaders and financial managers of this ministry be good stewards of the resources entrusted to them. Cause them to operate with integrity on every level of the organization, leaving no door open for Satan's entrance into their affairs. If any incompetence or failing on the part of this ministry has caused this financial shortfall, let the leaders acknowledge it and take corrective action without delay.

Your Word says that whatever I bind on earth will be bound in heaven, and whatever I loose on earth will be loosed in heaven (Matthew 18:18). Therefore, I bind every hindering, divisive, stingy, and unsupportive spirit that comes against this ministry to derail its efforts. I loose the spirit of generosity and decree that every plan, program, and project You have inspired will come to fruition in Your due season. In the name of Jesus, I pray. Amen.

My Pastor Has Sinned

✝ Lord, Pastor _____ has sinned against You and the congregation. Because he/she has confessed his/her sin, You promised to be faithful and just, to forgive him/her, and to cleanse him/her from all unrighteousness (1 John 1:9). I pray that You give the church's governing body the courage to impose appropriate sanctions, including counseling, extended time off from the ministry, and other accountability measures. Help Pastor _____ come to the full realization that he/she, like the congregation, must put on Your whole armor so he/she will be able to stand firm against all strategies and tricks of the devil (Ephesians 6:11).

Father, please do not let anyone from within or outside our congregation conclude from Pastor _____'s behavior that all Christians are hypocrites and masquerade as servants of righteousness (2 Corinthians 11:15). Let the church continue its work. Do not allow anyone to become discouraged and go back into the world because of this incident. Rather, cause everyone to understand that we are all capable of yielding to temptation if we do not hide Your Word in our hearts (Psalm 119:11) and meditate on it day and night (Joshua 1:8). Let pride, prayerlessness, and wrong priorities be far from Pastor _____ from this day forward. In the name of Jesus, I pray. Amen.

Lord, Protect Our Troops

✚ Father, You said that in the last days there would be wars and rumors of wars as nations rise against nations and kingdoms against kingdoms (Matthew 24:6-7). I pray a hedge of protection today for all of the men and women who have been sent to war areas to make the world a better place. Let each of them take the time to consider their eternal destiny and find peace in a personal relationship with You. I also pray for the peace, provision, and protection of their families. Comfort and encourage the troops in their hours of loneliness as only You can do because You are the God of all comfort (2 Corinthians 1:3).

Let the Christian soldiers be quick to share their faith with those who have not accepted Jesus as their Lord and Savior. I pray that the spiritual commitment of those who receive Christ during this crisis will be genuine and last throughout their lives.

Show Yourself strong on their behalf each day (2 Chronicles 16:9). Give Your angels charge of each military unit and keep the troops in all their ways (Psalm 91:11). Bring the war to a close, Father, and return the troops home.

I pray that You will extend Your mercy and peace to the citizens who reside in the war torn areas. Be with them and let them find refuge in You. In the name of Jesus, I pray. Amen.

Our Nation Is in Crisis

✚ Lord, our nation is in crisis, yet You have shown us a way out. You said that if Your people, who are called by Your name, will humble themselves and pray, seek Your face, and turn from their wicked ways, then You will hear from heaven, forgive their sin, and heal their land (2 Chronicles 7:14). I pray now, Father, that You will raise up an army of faithful prayer warriors who will stand in the gap for this nation so You will not allow us to be destroyed by our enemies, natural disasters, or other perils (Ezekiel 22:30-31).

Your Word declares that blessed is the nation whose God is the Lord (Psalm 33:12). Let us, as a nation, crown You King and Lord over our lives. Turn our hearts to You. Forgive us for passing laws that violate Your word, for embracing sexual perversion, and other sins as the norm.

Deliver us from the spirit of anxiety that plagues the people of this country. Your Word says that righteousness and peace have kissed each other (Psalm 85:10); help us comprehend the connection between being in right standing with You and being at peace. Send a spiritual revival now, Father.

Save our governmental leaders and let them seek Your wisdom in every situation for Your eyes are over the righteous, and Your ears are open unto their prayers (1 Peter 3:12). In the name of Jesus, I pray. Amen.

An Innocent Person Is Serving Time

✚ Father, _____ is serving time for a crime he/she did not commit. Just as You sent an angel and opened the prison doors for Your apostles who had been imprisoned (Acts 5:18-19), I pray that You send a legal angel to appeal _____'s case and deliver him/her from the bars of injustice. Let credible witnesses come forth to refute the accusations of the prosecutors; give _____ favor with the judge and jury. Your Word says that You detest those who acquit the guilty but condemn the innocent (Proverbs 17:15). Yes, those who make the innocent guilty by their false testimony will disappear. And those who use false testimony to pervert justice and tell lies to tear down the innocent will be no more (Isaiah 29:21).

Father, send chaplains, Christian workers, inmates, and others across _____'s path to minister Your Word to him/her and cause him/her to keep the faith for it is the substance of the thing he/she is hoping for and the evidence of things not seen (Hebrews 11:1). Do not let him/her become discouraged with the slow process of appeal. Give his/her attorney wisdom from on high and let him/her present an airtight case on _____'s behalf. Continue to remind _____ that You have plans for him/her; plans for prosperity and not harm; plans to give him/her hope and a future (Jeremiah 29:11). In the name of Jesus, I pray. Amen.

I'm Anxious About a Terrorist Attack

✚ Father, I have seen the destruction caused by terrorist acts. Satan wants to make me fear that one day I, or my family, may become victims of such senseless violence. I know that it is not Your will for me to live with anxiety for Your Word says be anxious for nothing (Philippians 4:6). Because You are my refuge and my fortress, I decree that I will not be afraid of the terrors of the night, nor fear the dangers of the day, nor dread the plague that stalks in darkness, nor the disaster that strikes at midday. Though a thousand fall at my side, though ten thousand are dying around me, these evils will not touch me or my family (Psalm 91:2,5-7).

Father, I pray that the leaders of this country will seek Your face in implementing international policies that do not inspire hate, but are just, fair, and righteous. You said that in righteousness we will be established; we will be far from oppression for we will not fear; and far from terror for it shall not come near us (Isaiah 54:14).

As a faithful intercessor, I stand in the gap for my country asking You to foil every plan of the terrorists. Cause the citizens of this nation to turn to You and not live in anxiety. Help us experience Your peace that passes our understanding and protects our hearts and our minds (Philippians 4:7). In the name of Jesus, I pray. Amen.

Thank God for the Victory

Father, I want to thank You for Your loving kindness and faithfulness to me. You have always been my strong tower. You are a shield for me, my glory, and the One who lifts up my head (Psalm 3:3). You have heard all of my petitions, You have seen my tears, and You have answered me according to Your divine purpose. I stand in awe of Your great power.

I do not have adequate words to express the depth of my gratitude to You for all You have done in providing for me, protecting me, comforting me, empowering me, and adopting me into Your family. I lift up to You the words of Mary, the mother of Your dear Son, Jesus:

"For the Mighty One is holy, and he has done great things for me.

He shows mercy from generation to generation to all who fear him.

His mighty arm has done tremendous things! He has scattered the proud and haughty ones. He has brought down princes from their thrones and exalted the humble. He has filled the hungry with good things and sent the rich away with empty hands" (Luke 1:49-53 NLT).

Thank You, Father, for never reneging on Your Word. It has been my anchor in the midst of every storm. I am eternally grateful to You for Your goodness and Your wonderful works. I exalt Your name above every name on the earth. In the name of Jesus, I pray. Amen!

Epilogue

I pray that the crisis prayers in this book have provided a practical model of how to pray and decree the Word of God in the midst of any trial, test, or temptation. Famed evangelist, R.A. Torrey, once said that the greatest secrets of prevailing prayer were to study the Word to find what God's will is as revealed in the promises, and then simply take these promises and spread them out before God in prayer with the absolutely unwavering expectation that He will do what He has promised in His Word.

God is standing ready to show Himself strong in your crisis now. He does not require you to come to Him with a long, theological discourse; all that He wants is a pure heart that will trust and believe His Word. Sometimes, a simple "Lord, help me!" may be all that is needed.

It behooves us to stay "prayed up" and prepared for the inevitable crises of life. It is foolish to wait until trouble shows up at our doorstep to begin this essential spiritual discipline. Live holy, pray without ceasing, and leave the results to God. Know that the effective, fervent prayer of a righteous man avails much (James 5:16).

My friend, do not tolerate prayerlessness in your life. Do not allow the stress of progress to dictate how much time you will sit at the feet of your Savior. Protect and crave those secluded times with the Father. Yes, you can pray on the run and even pray while running; however, to have true intimacy with the Father, you must integrate focused worship, listening, and note-taking into your prayers. Worship is—and requires—total preoccupation with the object of your affection. Effective worship is done in seclusion. "But thou, when thou prayest, enter into thy closet, and when thou hast shut thy door, pray to thy Father which is in secret; and thy Father which seeth in secret shall reward thee openly" (Matthew 6:6 KJV).

Get and stay on a consistent prayer track. Use the log on page 140 to monitor the amount of time you spend in secluded prayer during the course of a year. Hopefully, the Lord will be pleased with your record. You might also consider enlisting a trusted friend or mentor to join you in this project for mutual accountability and encouragement.

Let me challenge you once again, as I did in the prologue, to consider a verse from Joseph M. Scriven's popular hymn, "What a Friend We Have in Jesus."

> Have we trials and temptations?
> Is there trouble anywhere?
> We should never be discouraged,
> Take it to the Lord in prayer:
> Can we find a friend so faithful
> Who will all our sorrows share?
> Jesus knows our every weakness,
> Take it to the Lord in prayer.

The Difference

I got up early one morning
and rushed right into the day;
I had so much to accomplish,
I didn't have time to pray.

Problems just tumbled about me,
and heavier came each task.
Why doesn't God help me? I wondered,
He answered, "You didn't ask."

I wanted to see joy and beauty,
but the day toiled on, gray and bleak.
I wondered why God didn't show me,
He said, "But you didn't seek."

I tried to come into God's presence,
I used all my keys at the lock.
God gently and lovingly chided,
"My child, you didn't knock."

I woke up early this morning,
and paused before entering the day.
I had so much to accomplish
That I had to take time to pray.

Grace L. Naessens
(used with permission)

Daily Prayer Log

Indicate the number of minutes spent in secluded prayer each day.

	Jan	Feb	Mar	Apr	May	Jun	Jul	Aug	Sep	Oct	Nov	Dec
1												
2												
3												
4												
5												
6												
7												
8												
9												
10												
11												
12												
13												
14												
15												
16												
17												
18												
19												
20												
21												
22												
23												
24												
25												
26												
27												
28												
29												
30		▮										
31			▮		▮		▮		▮		▮	

Other Books by Deborah Smith Pegues

30 Days to Taming Your Tongue
Certified behavioral consultant Deborah Pegues uses short stories, anecdotes, soul-searching questions, and scripturally based personal affirmations in this 30-day devotional that is tongue-and-life-changing.

30 Days to Taming Your Tongue Workbook
This interactive 30-day guide to the bestselling *30 Days to Taming Your Tongue* will give you ways to apply the book's advice to your circumstances; ideas and plans to overcome negative speech patterns; and words from Scripture to reinforce the changes you're making.

30 Days to Taming Your Finances
Sharing her expertise as a certified public accountant, Deborah Pegues sheds light on the emotional and practical side of organizing, spending, saving, and sharing finances wisely and the freedom this brings to life.

30 Days to Taming Your Stress
Deborah Pegues helps you exchange your stress for peace in just one month's time as you learn how to extend grace, meditate on Scripture, and increase your sense of purpose, contentment, and freedom.

Supreme Confidence
This is a powerful guide to overcoming the core fears that rob people of life's fullness. *Supreme Confidence* uses strategies such as resisting intimidation, resting in God's Word, and remembering past victories to provide an effective plan of attack on self-doubt.